Y0-CDF-414

SCIENTIFIC
AMERICAN™ *Critical Anthologies on Environment and Climate*™

CRITICAL PERSPECTIVES ON
POLITICS AND
THE ENVIRONMENT

Edited by Rick Adair

The Rosen Publishing Group, Inc., New York

Published in 2007 by The Rosen Publishing Group, Inc.
29 East 21st Street, New York, NY 10010

Copyright © 2007 by Scientific American, Inc. All rights reserved.

No part of this book may be reproduced in any form or format without
permission in writing from the publisher, except by a reviewer.

The articles in this book first appeared in the pages of *Scientific American*, as
follows: "The Treaty That Worked—Almost" by W. Wayt Gibbs, September
1995; "Debt and the Environment" by David Pearce, Neil Adger, David
Maddison, and Dominic Moran, June 1995; "Risk Analysis and Management"
by M. Granger Morgan, July 1993; "Shaping the Future" by Steven W. Popper,
Robert J. Lempert, and Steven C. Bankes, April 2005; "Sound Science?" by
Marguerite Holloway, August 1993; "Wetlands" by Jon A. Kusler, William
J. Mitsch, and Joseph S. Larson, January 1994; "Endangered: One Endangered
Species Act" by Tim Beardsley, March 1995; "The Arctic Oil and Wildlife
Refuge" by W. Wayt Gibbs, May 2001; "Trade Rules" by Marguerite Holloway,
August 1998; "The Case for Free Trade" by Jagdish Bhagwati, November 1993;
"The Perils of Free Trade" by Herman E. Daly, November 1993; "Rules of the
Game" by Tim Beardsley, April 2000; "Ten Years of the Chornobyl Era" by
Yuri M. Shcherbak, April 1996; "The Case for Electric Vehicles" by Daniel
Sperling, November 1996; "Under the Microscope" by Daniel G. Dupont,
December 2002; and "Acting Locally" by David Appell, June 2003.

First Edition

Library of Congress Cataloging-in-Publication Data

Critical perspectives on politics and the environment/edited by Rick Adair.—
1st ed.
    p. cm.—(Scientific American critical anthologies on environment and climate)
Includes bibliographical references and index.
ISBN 1-4042-0823-2 (library binding)
1. Environmentalism. 2. Environmental policy. I. Adair, Rick. II. Series.

GE195.P65 2007
333.7—dc22

2005031480

Manufactured in the United States of America

On the cover: On September 20, 2005, protesters in Washington, D.C., urged
members of the U.S. Congress to keep the Arctic National Wildlife Refuge
closed to oil drilling.

CONTENTS

Introduction

The evidence is mounting that human activities are warming the earth at an alarming rate, a warming that could alter social and economic fabrics around the world as its environmental effects play out. To the extent that humans are responsible for this danger, it is natural to seek a remedy. But a problem as big as rapid global climate change seems beyond the abilities of individuals to solve. Rather, the solution—if there is one—likely lies with governments, which can change policies and mandate behaviors with the stroke of a pen.

However, arriving at the stage where laws and policies are changed requires politics, which is the art or science concerned with managing or affecting governmental policy. In practice, politics is "the art of the possible" of what can actually be achieved, according to Otto von Bismarck (1815–1898), prime minister of Prussia and first chancellor of the German Empire. But a more recent and cynical perspective, from American (Canadian-born) economist John Kenneth Galbraith (1908–), holds that "politics is not the art of the possible. It consists in choosing between the disastrous and the unpalatable."

In the case of combating global warming, governments seem to adopt versions of Galbraith's outlook. The European Union says that doing nothing now to address global warming would be disastrous, and so it has taken definite steps laid out in the Kyoto Protocol that nibble away at the problem. The protocol, an amendment to the United Nations Framework Convention on Climate Change, mandates cuts in the greenhouse gas emissions blamed for global warming. The treaty went into effect on February 16, 2005.

The United States and Australia, on the other hand, have refused to ratify the Kyoto Protocol. They say the steps it mandates to reduce emissions would be disastrous for their economies. Instead, they have proposed fixes based on technologies yet to be developed and prescribed courses of action that are voluntary.

Nevertheless, support for the Kyoto Protocol is emerging within the United States among individuals, cities, and states, as David Appell describes in his June 2003 article "Acting Locally," included in this anthology. This support flows from a tradition of environmentalism that first burst onto the scene in the 1960s and flowered in the following decade with the creation of the Environmental Protection Agency, Earth Day, and several key legislative acts aimed at protecting the environment.

Before these modern developments, there was an older conservation movement that recognized that destroying nature could have dire effects on urban living. One of the earliest examples of this is Boston's creation of a municipal water system in 1652 to protect its water supplies. This awareness became heightened beginning in the mid-nineteenth century, according to the preface of the Library of Congress's American Memory online exhibition *The Evolution of the Conservation Movement, 1850–1920*. It emerged as a "complex, broadly popular political and cultural movement, based largely on a growing appreciation among newly-urbanized Americans for the importance of nature as an economic, aesthetic, and spiritual resource." The driving force of the movement came from the conviction that "nature's resources were increasingly imperiled," which led to public and private efforts intended to ensure "the wise and scientific use of natural resources, and the preservation of wildlife and of landscapes of great natural beauty."

Diverse trends and attitudes came together to develop the movement's ideals and policies. This diversity was seen in the debate during the early 1900s over the building of a dam on the Tuolumne River in Hetch Hetchy Valley in Yosemite National Park to provide San Francisco with water.

Preservationist members of the conservation movement battled utilitarian members, but lost (O'Shaughnessy Dam was completed in 1923). However, it galvanized the preservationists (including John Muir and Will Colby of the Sierra Club) to campaign for national park protection, an effort that led to the creation of the National Park Service.

The conservation movement nudged government into the role of nature's steward, one that preserved wilderness but also harnessed natural forces. The Library of Congress exhibition notes several accomplishments of the government between 1850 and 1920: the development of the national park system and the world's first national park (Yellowstone), the establishment of the national forest system and the Forest Service, the institution of natural resource management and large-scale irrigation projects, and the establishment of a national wildlife refuge system. People of this era also saw the presidency of Theodore Roosevelt, who made conservation a cornerstone of his administration.

Following this period, governmental policy continued on a course of protecting natural resources on the one hand, and using them to benefit the public on the other. In the 1930s, during President Franklin D. Roosevelt's administration, the Tennessee Valley Authority in the Southeast and the Bonneville Power

Administration in the Northwest were created to manage the massive system of dams that harnessed rivers and used them to generate electricity.

The pressure on undeveloped areas to accommodate a population surge after World War II (1939–1945) brought a new awareness of the strains on nature and concerns about air and water pollution, radiation, and pesticide poisoning. Biologist Rachel Carson's influential book *Silent Spring* (1962), about the dangers of some pesticide practices, set the stage for environmentalism as the successor of conservation and "helped ignite a generation of environmental action," as former vice president Al Gore wrote in an online comment.

In addition to the traditional tool of public opinion, the environmental movement expanded its influence into courtrooms with the 1965 *Scenic Hudson Preservation Conference v. Federal Power Commission* ruling (also known as the Storm King ruling). In 1963, Consolidated Edison, a New York utility, made public its plans to build a power plant on Storm King Mountain near the Hudson River. For the first time, a conservation group (Scenic Hudson Preservation Conference) was allowed to sue to protect the public interest without having an economic interest in the matter. The Scenic Hudson Preservation Conference was deemed to be an injured party entitled to a review of a Federal Power Commission's license for a pumped-storage hydroelectric project.

The politicians were quick to catch on. Whereas speeches and legislation in the early 1960s rarely mentioned the environment except when referring to natural resources, nature became a vital campaign and political issue later in the decade. This is also reflected in the variety of laws passed in the ensuing years: the Water Quality, Noise Control, and Solid Waste Disposal acts (1965); Clean Air acts (1963, 1970); National Environmental Policy Act (1969); Water Pollution Control, Coastal Zone Management, Ocean Dumping, and Marine Mammal Protection acts (1972); Endangered Species Act (1973); and Safe Drinking Water Act (1974).

The articles gathered in this anthology examine facets of the relationship between politics and environmentalism. Politics serves at times as the environment's righteous, defending sword, and at other times as a cudgel, battering the edifice of regulations and laws built to protect the environment. Chapter 1 starts with an example of a wildly popular international treaty to protect the ozone layer that nonetheless had its share of problems. The chapter then examines whether third-world debt guarantees environmental problems and ends with a look at methods (one standard, the other cutting-edge) that policymakers use to help craft solutions to environmental problems. Chapter 2 looks at assaults on the environment and on environmental regulation. Chapter 3 focuses on the relationship between trade and environmental concerns. Chapter 4 wraps up with a look at current and future problems, and possible solutions. —*RA*

1 Myths and Methods

The following article illustrates the difficulties international environmental treaties can have, even when they are extremely successful and popular. As W. Wayt Gibbs, a senior writer and member of the board of editors at Scientific American *magazine, says, "International environmental treaties tend to be poorly focused, rarely ratified and hardly enforced." Succeeding in all of these aspects requires an unusual degree of agreement among powerful nations about a problem and about the need to enforce remedies.*

The 1987 Montreal Protocol is just such an agreement. It mandates phasing out several compounds identified as harmful to Earth's ozone layer, including common refrigerants. Yet, although United Nations secretary-general Kofi Annan in 2000 praised it as "perhaps the most successful environmental agreement to date," the growing pains described in Gibbs's 1995 article threatened to derail it. Nevertheless, it has ambled forward with the help of financial aid to countries having trouble complying (most notably Russia) and several amendments.

Although it could be held up as a model for what can be expected from the now-ratified Kyoto Protocol, there are several key differences. Most significant, alternatives exist for the compounds targeted by the Montreal Protocol, but as yet there are no widely accepted replacements for fossil fuels, which contribute most strongly to greenhouse gas production. —RA

"The Treaty That Worked—Almost"
by W. Wayt Gibbs
Scientific American, September 1995

As a rule, international environmental treaties tend to be poorly focused, rarely ratified and hardly enforced. One notable exception—so far—is the Montreal Protocol, a 1987 agreement ratified by 149 countries to phase out production of the chlorofluorocarbons (CFCs) that scientists have convincingly implicated in the destruction of the earth's ozone layer.

But a series of recent busts by federal authorities has revealed a thriving black market for illicit CFCs that threatens to slow significantly the transition to less harmful substitutes in the U.S. Although officials assert that they are on top of the situation, they admit they do not know the scope of the illegal imports and cannot predict their growth: agents estimate that in Miami the chemicals are second only to drugs in dollar value. Some warn that contraband CFCs will pose a larger problem for Europe.

CFCs are still used as refrigerants in some 100 million cars, 160 million home refrigerators, five million commercial refrigerators and food display cases, and 70,000 air conditioners for large buildings in the U.S. But since 1986, production of new CFCs in this country has fallen 75 percent, thanks to the Montreal Protocol; on New Year's Day, 1996, it will cease altogether. Meanwhile federal excise taxes on new and imported CFCs, which cost only about $2 per pound to make, have grown to $5.35 per pound and continue to rise.

The dramatically shrinking supply and sharply rising taxes are supposed to push people to replace or convert their cooling equipment so that it runs on less harmful substitutes, which are now widely available. But that transition is going slowly, and the skyrocketing prices for CFCs create a huge incentive for smuggling. "It's very lucrative," says Keith S. Prager, a U.S. Customs agent in Miami. "You can make millions."

Indeed, six people in four separate cases have been charged with attempting to smuggle a total of 8.166 million pounds of CFCs into the U.S. without paying the tax. (Five of the defendants were convicted and may face prison terms.) If sold at market price, that quantity could net some $40 million.

"We don't really know how much is coming in," admits David Lee of the Environmental Protection Agency's stratospheric protection division. But eight million pounds is equivalent to 10 percent of the U.S.'s total legal production of CFCs this year. Lee reports that "Du Pont and AlliedSignal, two major CFC producers, are complaining that they simply cannot move their inventory, even though you would expect a lot of demand." The market, the companies charge, is flooded with contraband.

If, as some worry, the government is no more effective at halting CFC smuggling than at interdicting drugs, then 10 times as much material gets through as is intercepted. That fear is fueled by the fact that the smugglers caught so far all labeled their cargo properly as refrigerant but falsely claimed that it was destined for ports outside the U.S. Probably many others disguise CFC cylinders as those of other gases; they will be harder to catch. If the analogy between CFCs and drugs is valid, in 1996 the black market may completely counteract the effects of the ban.

There are, however, good reasons to suspect that the worst will not happen. "Many businesses have stockpiled enough CFCs to keep their equipment running for years," says Edward W. Dooley of the Air Conditioning and Refrigeration Institute. "And the market for domestically recycled freon [which is tax-exempt] is growing like topsy."

More important, CFCs are generally sold to businesses, which are unlikely to invite a run-in with the Internal Revenue Service by knowingly buying such goods. And few building managers will risk damaging $100,000 chiller units by refilling them with coolant from an unknown source. Analysis of seized illegal CFC-12, for instance, has revealed that some samples contain up to 50 percent more moisture and 1,000 percent more contaminants than the industry standard, points out David Stirpe, executive director of the Alliance for Responsible Atmospheric Policy.

"We're more concerned with the automotive sector," says Tom Land, who is directing the CFC phaseout for the EPA. "Fly-by-night mechanics working out of the backs of trucks are not too concerned with purity. Cheap, illegal CFCs might seem too good of a deal on the street for some technicians to pass up." He points to one automotive air-conditioning shop owner who was recently charged with smuggling 60,000 pounds of CFCs from Mexico.

The EPA has a potentially powerful weapon against such small-time customers for bootleg CFCs: their competitors. The agency has set up an 800 number as a tip line and has been passing on leads to the IRS. "It's a dog-eat-dog world, and if someone thinks their competitor is obtaining CFCs at low cost without paying tax, they are going to fink," Land says. "We've been getting an average of three tips a week."

Europe may have a harder time making the Montreal Protocol stick. Customs officials believe that many of the illicit CFCs entering the U.S. are produced in former Soviet bloc countries. In May, Russia, Belarus, Ukraine, Poland and Bulgaria all asked for extensions, citing economic difficulties. Many in the environmental community expect President Boris N. Yeltsin to announce formally that Russia is not complying with the treaty. It is not clear how other countries would react.

If Russia falters, the rest of Europe may find it difficult to comply as well. Smuggling is always easier by land than by sea. And despite the European Union's adoption of a CFC manufacturing ban one year earlier than the U.S., the U.S. has made more progress in switching to CFC alternatives, EPA officials say. A number of American experts believe European regulators may soon face quite a scare as they realize that the transition will take longer than expected. The resultant spike in demand could lead to rampant growth in the black market for CFCs.

Whether governments can bring the traffic in CFCs under control may well determine the future of the Montreal Protocol. "We've been working under the assumption that the ozone issue is solved," says Joseph Mendelson of Friends of the Earth. "But none of our models predicting when CFC releases will peak and when the ozone hole will close up take into account smuggling and large countries that don't comply." Those details may force planners back to the drawing board.

Controversy persists to this day over whether loans to developing nations lead to a "spiral of debt and environmental degradation," a notion the authors of the following article say is far from proven. The issue is an important one because it has a bearing on how such countries can be part of the solution in dealing with global warming rather than part of the problem.

One argument holds that domestic policy changes made in the debtor country to provide cash for loan payments lead to problems that include increased pollution and accelerated depletion of natural resources. While acknowledging that employment, economic growth, prices, and income distribution have suffered under the burden imposed by debt repayment, the authors insist that there is "scant empirical evidence" to support a connection between debt and the environment. In fact, they suggest that in some cases, the "fiscal discipline" arising from the debt may "rein in environmentally harmful spending." What seems clear from the article is that it would be dangerous to assume that debt repayment will always cause environmental degradation, which has many causes, and that each case must be considered separately. —RA

"Debt and the Environment"
by David Pearce, Neil Adger, David Maddison, and Dominic Moran
Scientific American, June 1995

Some environmentalists claim that loans to developing nations have led to a spiral of debt and environmental degradation. According to their argument, the domestic policy changes that countries make to generate cash for loan payments—often under duress from the International Monetary Fund or the World Bank—hasten the depletion of natural resources, increase pollution and harm the poor, who may be uprooted in ways that cause further environmental damage. Many critics also contend that lenders should write off the loans because the money, in any case, is effectively irretrievable and because relieving countries of repayment obligations will encourage "sustainable development."

Although economic theory does not automatically render repayment incompatible with full employment, steady prices, economic growth or an equitable distribution of income, in reality these goals have suffered. As a result, most debtor nations continue to rely on outside funds, even though additional loans only make their predicament sharper. Whether the environment has also been harmed directly is less clear. There is scant empirical evidence to suggest that the connection between debt and the environment is significant. Indeed, in some cases, the fiscal discipline imposed by debt may rein in environmentally harmful spending.

The debt crisis has its origins in the oil-price shock of 1973, when energy prices roughly doubled in a matter of months. Commercial banks, flush with deposits from oil producers, were eager to lend money to developing countries, especially as they took it as an article of faith that nations always repay their debts. The borrowers, meanwhile, were glad to see money plentifully available at low interest rates. In 1979, when oil prices doubled again, industrial nations raised interest rates to slow their economies and thus reduce inflation. This action spurred a global recession that stifled demand for the raw materials developing nations were producing.

As interest rates rose, debtor nations faced higher payments on their outstanding loans but had less income with which to pay. Many found themselves unable to meet their current obligations, much less get new loans. Repayment became an overriding policy objective, affecting both government and private spending, because only wide-ranging changes in developing economies could generate the needed hard currency. A large fraction of many countries' earnings continues to be earmarked for the repayment of debt.

Exports at Any Cost

The most commonly held view linking debt with environmental degradation is known as the exports promotion hypothesis. To earn foreign exchange with which to repay international debts, a country must divert resources away from production of domestic goods to sectors generating commodities for export. According to this theory, production of goods for export causes more environmental degradation than does production of goods for domestic consumption, and so debt repayment harms the environment. There is no a priori reason to expect such a difference, but some environmentalists contend that it still does occur. They point to the possibility, for example, that countries will raze their forests for tropical timbers or to open up land for cash crops.

Nevertheless, statistical analysis of data from many developing countries suggests that national income and commodity prices have just as much influence on levels of exports as debt does. Raymond Gullison of Princeton University and Elizabeth C. Losos, now at the Smithsonian Tropical Research Institute, examined the effect of debt on timber exports from Bolivia, Brazil, Chile, Costa Rica, Paraguay, Peru, Colombia, Ecuador and Mexico but found only minimal correlations overall. Furthermore, in Paraguay, the only country on which debt apparently did have a significant effect, increased debt was associated with reduced production.

More recently James R. Kahn of the University of Tennessee and Judith A. MacDonald of Lehigh University found more concrete evidence of a correlation between debt and deforestation, although they also found that country-specific factors played a strong role. They estimate that reducing a country's debt by $1 billion might cut annual deforestation by between 51 and 930 square kilometers. Brazil currently clears more than 25,000 square kilometers a year and Indonesia more than 6,000.

Deforestation is only one aspect of environmental degradation in developing countries. Unfortunately, the impact of indebtedness on other environmental indicators such as pollution, biodiversity or depletion of other resources has not been tested.

Reductions in Domestic Spending

Evidence for or against other mechanisms by which debt repayment might damage the environment is largely anecdotal and speculative. Some observers have placed blame on reductions in domestic spending by nations that shifted money toward financing their debt. In sub-Saharan Africa, outlays for health, education and other public services decreased by more than 40 percent during the 1980s, in parallel with a sharp rise in money spent on repayment of debt. Yet the effects on the environment remain unclear.

Cuts in government spending may fall on measures designed specifically to enhance the environment, such as schemes to improve water quality and sanitation. On the other hand, some cuts may cancel large capital projects, including the construction of dams and roads, that have often been criticized for causing environmental devastation far in excess of any financial returns they may bring. Elimination of roadbuilding programs in the Brazilian Amazon, for instance, may have helped curtail deforestation. From a theoretical point of view, then, reductions in government spending can act to either improve or degrade the environment.

The same uncertainty emerges when one looks specifically at the effect of debt on spending for environmental protection. Some economists assert that environmental quality should increase with national income. (Their claim, called the Kuznets curve effect, grows out of the observation by Simon Kuznets, who won the Nobel Prize in Economics in 1971, that richer nations have more equitable income distributions.) Conversely, a nation faced with a huge debt is likely to divert money from the environment to more pressing problems.

But does the relaxing of environmental standards inevitably increase pollution? Perhaps not. Many debtor nations have probably always spent little on protecting the environment, and so decreases in spending could have a minimal impact. Moreover, a country repaying debt might not be able to afford high standards for pollution control, but it also might be unable to afford goods whose production damages the environment.

It is conceivable, however, that absent or unenforced environmental regulations or their lax enforcement might also make for the establishment of "pollution havens"—a situation that many claim has occurred in the Maquiladora export-processing zone of northern Mexico. Supposedly, U.S. companies have been attracted to this area because of the lower environmental standards. Yet a 1992 study by Gene M. Grossman and Alan B. Krueger of Princeton found little statistical support for this claim. They argue that low wages and easy access to U.S. markets spurred investment. Thus, the net effect that reduced domestic spending has on pollution and resource degradation is not clear.

In addition to causing ecologically unsound export drives or budget cuts, excessive debt can potentially exacerbate local practices that already put the environment at risk. Diversion of money to debt service has triggered massive unemployment in many countries, sometimes prompting poor people to migrate in search either of work or land on which to grow food to live. Marginal lands and fisheries whose ownership was indeterminate have often attracted migrants, until the topsoil or fish have been depleted.

Overexploitation would have come about even without these evils, however; the inefficiency results from the lack of established rules for access to land, water and other resources. Many indebted countries seem to be characterized by the hallmarks of shared resources, a high level of migratory subsistence farming, overgrazing and declining yields. Ill-defined or non-existent ownership has often precipitated the exhaustion of land. The enforcement of property rights would in many cases have prevented overuse by giving people incentives for proper husbandry.

Structural Adjustment

Nations that face increasing poverty are often forced to try to secure additional loans. As a condition of attaining this money, heavily indebted countries have often had to make "structural adjustments" to their economies: eliminating subsidies, removing tariffs and privatizing government-owned enterprises. These reforms aim to help them grow out of indebtedness by removing glaring economic inefficiencies.

Some observers contend that these "conditionality" programs let governments push ahead with policy changes that were previously impossible, by putting multilateral institutions in the position of political lightning rods. Others think conditionality makes all objectives, including environmental ones, subordinate to debt repayment. Systematic cuts in such vital services as education, health and food (which would typically be higher on a government's list of priorities than the environment) give some weight to the latter view. If it is correct, one would expect to find environmental repercussions in countries that have received significant structural adjustment loans.

The evidence is equivocal. Case studies of conditionality programs of the International Monetary Fund in Mexico, Ivory Coast and Thailand, sponsored by the World Wildlife Fund International, suggest that structural adjustment programs have on balance benefited the environment. In Thailand the removal of indirect irrigation subsidies has helped reduce waterlogging and salinization. Yet in Malawi, which has undertaken four International Monetary Fund restructuring packages and six World Bank structural adjustment loans since 1979, the Overseas Development Institute found many more negative results than positive ones.

In the Philippines, a study by the World Resources Institute found that structural adjustments undertaken in the 1980s encouraged overexploitation of natural resources and resulted in increased emissions of pollutants, concentrated pollution and congestion in urban areas.

Whether the consequences for the environment are good or bad seems to depend a great deal on the particular provisions of the loan agreement and on the individual circumstances of a country or even a region within a country. In Ivory Coast, controls on food prices and subsidies for fertilizers and pesticides have been minimized. These changes could cause the abandonment of some environmentally harmful farming practices, but lower yields may also bring about cultivation of remaining forestland. In Malawi, currency devaluation and agricultural reforms have contributed to an increase in tobacco farming and created incentives for planting such crops as cotton and hybrid maize, which tend to be grown in a manner that promotes erosion. Malawi's case cannot be taken entirely at face value, however: large-scale migration of refugees from Mozambique has placed an unprecedented strain on the country's resources, unrelated to structural reform.

In other parts of the world, structural adjustment appears to have helped the environment. Agricultural subsidies, which adjustment programs curtail, have played a significant role in deforestation and the destruction of soil in areas subject to erosion. Until the late 1980s, for example, Brazil gave tax credits for cutting down forests, and it subsidized loans for crops and livestock development. These government incentives typically covered more than two thirds of the cost of cattle ranches, which reportedly accounted for 72 percent of all deforestation in the Brazilian Amazon up to 1980. Toward the end of the 1980s, after the government abandoned many of the clearance subsidies, deforestation slowed. Other evidence from Brazilian Amazonia also supports the idea that public expenditure on infrastructure, such as on roads, is linked to migration onto marginal land that results in deforestation, erosion and other deleterious effects.

Reduction of subsidies for energy use could also have a salutary effect on the environments of developing nations. Anwar M. Shah and Bjorn K. Larsen of the World Bank have calculated that total world energy subsidies amounted to $230 billion in 1990. Eliminating them could cut emissions of carbon dioxide (the main greenhouse gas) by 9.5 percent and improve prospects for economic growth by freeing the money for other uses. Indeed, the developing world has many resources that could be used more efficiently, thereby enabling nations to repay foreign debts without reducing domestic consumption.

Structural adjustment programs can potentially prove beneficial in another way as well. Recent structural loans have been made on the condition that governments clarify land-ownership questions. Such arrangements should reduce somewhat the environmental degradation brought about by shared use of land that seems to belong to anybody and to nobody in particular.

Debt Forgiveness

At best, then, evidence on the extent to which environmental degradation in the developing world can be attributed to debt repayment remains inconclusive. Nevertheless, given the fact that debt repayment is largely to blame for the drastic reductions in per capita spending on social programs in these countries, cannot a strong case be made in favor of debt forgiveness? In secondary markets, debt of developing countries often changes hands at a fraction of its contractual value. This steep discount is an indication that the commercial banks expect that the loans will never be repaid in full.

Banks do not simply write off the uncollectible debt, for two simple reasons. First is the problem of moral hazard: forgiveness may encourage countries to get into more debt in the expectation that it, too, would be forgiven. Such profligacy would obviously jeopardize other assets held by the banks. The second reason is uncertainty. There is a slight possibility that unexpected favorable developments will eventually enable developing countries to repay more of their debts, and so it is not in the interest of any bank to deprive itself of the opportunity of benefiting from any windfall to the borrower.

Conversely, a reduction of part of the contractual debt that the debtor is not expected to repay anyway

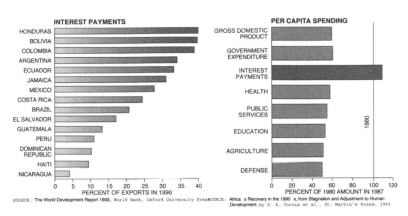

Scope of debt problems can be seen in data from Latin American (*left*) and Africa (*right*). Interest payments on Latin American debt consume as much as 40 percent of nations' earnings, leaving less money to pay for needed imports. Nations in sub-Saharan Africa have slashed all government expenditures except for debt, leaving their citizens considerably worse off.

is of little value. It neither reduces current cash requirements nor makes it easier to get new loans. When Bolivia spent $34 million to buy back $308 million in bonds in 1988, the price of the remaining bonds rose from six to 11 cents on the dollar. As a result, the real value of outstanding debt declined from $40.2 million ($670 million at six cents on the dollar) to $39.8 million (362 million at 11 cents), less than $400,000.

The same problem afflicts other debt-reduction mechanisms, such as debt-for-nature swaps. Until 1992, 17 countries had participated in such swaps: donors spent $16 million to retire nearly $100 million of debts in developing countries in return for the establishment of national parks and other environmental improvements. Although the swaps do preserve some environmentally vulnerable regions, the large nominal reduction barely touches nations' real burdens. Indeed, they may even have increased expected repayments.

No Easy Path

It seems, then, that excessive debt inevitably causes radical restructuring of a nation's economy. Because economic policies play a crucial part in determining how natural resources are used, the environment is bound to be affected. Yet it is very difficult to predict whether any particular change will cause harm or prevent it.

Such links as exist between indebtedness and damage to the environment stem largely from structural adjustment programs and their requirement that money be reallocated from government subsidies and other spending to repayment. Even then, most environmental degradation in the developing world probably has causes other than the servicing of debt. Structural adjustment is more justly criticized on humanitarian grounds than on environmental ones. Instead of alleviating unemployment and equitably redistributing income, price reforms—particularly elimination of subsidies for food and fuel—have fallen most heavily on the poor.

Given that the connection between debt repayment and environmental degradation is tenuous at best, attempting to improve the environment by debt forgiveness would probably be futile. The most effective way to confront pollution, deforestation and similar problems in debtor nations is to establish individual ownership of resources that are currently open to all, to end environmentally damaging subsidies, to institute market-based pollution-control mechanisms (in which those who produce toxic substances pay for their effects) and to make direct payments where necessary to preserve environmental assets of global significance. Undoubtedly, the flow of funds from the South to the North causes poverty, malnourishment, ill health and lack of educational opportunity. These consequences make a compelling case for debt relief. But such aid is not a panacea for environmental degradation.

The Authors

David Pearce, Neil Adger, David Maddison and Dominic Moran investigate the interplay between economic forces and the environment. Pearce is director of the Center for Social and Economic Research on Global Environment (CSERGE) at University College London and professor of economics at the university. He has headed several international working groups on economics and the environment. Among his hobbies are porcelain collecting and birdwatching. Adger is a senior research associate at CSERGE at the University of East Anglia. Maddison, a research fellow at CSERGE, teaches at University College and conducts research on the socioeconomic effects of climatic change. Moran, a research associate at CSERGE, investigates the valuation of environmental assets and the economics of biodiversity.

The next two articles discuss techniques used to analyze hazards, measure the associated risks, and decide what to do about the hazards based on the risks. Although some might consider risk analysis a dry topic, it is fundamental in setting environmental policy. Indeed, risk analysis underlies any modern policymaking effort, particularly when it involves choosing from various trade-offs.

After its establishment in 1970, the Environmental Protection Agency helped adapt existing risk analysis methods to address complex environmental hazards. These methods started as straightforward technical assessments in which every aspect was assumed to be per-fectly known. Over time, the methods included information about what was less known by using statistics.

In the following article, M. Granger Morgan describes enhancements to risk analysis, including consideration of public participation, perception, and risk evaluation, all of which he says can be as important as the technical *assessment. The article draws in part on the study performed at the behest of the White House Office of Science and Technology Policy by Morgan and his colleagues in the Engineering and Public Policy Department at Carnegie Mellon University in Pittsburgh, Pennsylvania. They applied this integrated approach in a study of how federal agencies could rank the risks they manage. —RA*

"Risk Analysis and Management"
by M. Granger Morgan
Scientific American, July 1993

Americans live longer and healthier lives today than at any time in their history. Yet they seem preoccupied with risks to health, safety and the environment. Many advocates, such as industry representatives promoting unpopular technology or Environmental Protection Agency staffers defending its regulatory agenda, argue that the public has a bad sense of perspective. Americans, they say, demand that enormous efforts be directed at small but scary-sounding risks while virtually ignoring larger, more commonplace ones.

Other evidence, however, suggests that citizens are eminently sensible about risks they face. Recent decades have witnessed precipitous drops in the rate and social acceptability of smoking, widespread shifts toward low-fat, high-fiber diets, dramatic improvements in automobile safety and the passage of mandatory seat belt laws—all steps that reduce the chance of untimely demise at little cost.

My experience and that of my colleagues indicate that the public can be very sensible about risk when companies, regulators and other institutions give it the opportunity. Laypeople have different, broader definitions of risk, which in important respects can be more rational than the narrow ones used by experts. Furthermore, risk management is, fundamentally, a question of values. In a democratic society, there is no acceptable way to make these choices without involving the citizens who will be affected by them.

The public agenda is already crowded with unresolved issues of certain or potential hazards such as AIDS, asbestos in schools and contaminants in food and drinking water. Meanwhile scientific and social developments are bringing new problems—global warming, genetic engineering and others—to the fore. To meet the challenge that these issues pose, risk analysts and managers will have to change their agenda for evaluating dangers to the general welfare; they will also have to adopt new communication styles and learn from the populace rather than simply trying to force information on it.

While public trust in risk management has declined, ironically the discipline of risk analysis has matured. It is now possible to examine potential hazards in a rigorous, quantitative fashion and thus to give people and their representatives facts on which to base essential personal and political decisions.

Risk analysts start by dividing hazards into two parts: exposure and effect. Exposure studies look at the ways in which a person (or, say, an ecosystem or a piece of art) might be subjected to change; effects studies examine what may happen once that exposure has manifested itself. Investigating the risks of lead for inner-city children, for example, might start with exposure studies to learn how old, flaking house paint releases lead into the environment and how children build up the substance in their bodies by inhaling dust or ingesting dirt. Effects studies might then attempt to determine the reduction in academic performance attributable to specific amounts of lead in the blood.

Exposure to a pollutant or other hazard may cause a complex chain of events leading to one of a number of effects, but analysts have found that the overall result can be modeled by a function that assigns a single number to any given exposure level. A simple, linear relation, for instance, accurately describes the average cancer risk incurred by smokers: 10 cigarettes a day generally increase the chance of contracting lung cancer by a factor of 25; 20 cigarettes a day increase it by a factor of 50. For other risks, however, a simple dose-response function is not appropriate, and more complex models must be used.

The study of exposure and effects is fraught with uncertainty. Indeed, uncertainty is at the heart of the definition of risk. In many cases, the risk may be well understood in a statistical sense but still be uncertain at the level of individual events. Insurance companies cannot predict whether any single driver will be killed or injured in an accident, even though they can estimate the annual number of crash-related deaths and injuries in the U.S. with considerable precision.

For other risks, such as those involving new technologies or those in which bad outcomes occur only rarely, uncertainty enters the calculations at a higher level—overall probabilities as well as individual events are unpredictable. If good actuarial data are not available, analysts must find other methods to estimate the likelihood of exposure and subsequent effects. The development of risk assessment during the past two decades has been in large part the story of finding ways to determine the extent of risks that have little precedent.

In one common technique, failure mode and effect analysis, workers try to identify all the events that might help cause a system to break down. Then they compile as complete a description as possible of the routes by which those events could lead to a failure (for instance, a chemical tank might release its contents either because a weld cracks and the tank ruptures or because an electrical short causes the cooling system to stop, allowing the contents to overheat and eventually explode). Although enumerating all possible routes to failure may sound like a simple task, it is difficult to exhaust all the alternatives. Usually a system must be described several times in different ways before analysts are confident that they have grasped its intricacies, and even then it is often impossible to be sure that all avenues have been identified.

Once the failure modes have been enumerated, a fault tree can aid in estimating the likelihood of any given mode. This tree graphically depicts how the subsystems of an object depend on one another and how the failure of one part affects key operations. Once the fault tree has been constructed, one need only estimate the probability that individual elements will fail to find the chance that the entire system will cease to function under a particular set of circumstances. Norman C. Rasmussen of the Massachusetts Institute of Technology was among the first to use the method on a large scale when he directed a study of nuclear reactor safety in 1975. Although specific details of his estimates were disputed, fault trees are now used routinely in the nuclear industry and other fields.

Boeing applies fault-tree analysis to the design of large aircraft. Company engineers have identified and remedied a number of potential problems, such as vulnerabilities caused by routing multiple control lines through the same area. Alcoa workers recently used fault trees to examine the safety of their large furnaces. On the basis of their findings, the company revised its safety standards to mandate the use of programmable logic controllers for safety-critical controls. They also instituted rigorous testing of automatic shut-off valves for leaks and added alarms that warn operators to close manual isolation valves during shutdown periods.

The company estimates that these changes have reduced the likelihood of explosions by a factor of 20. Major chemical companies such as Du Pont, Monsanto and Union Carbide have also employed the technique in designing processes for chemical plants, in deciding where to build plants and in evaluating the risks of transporting chemicals.

In addition to dealing with uncertainty about the likelihood of an event such as the breakdown of a crucial piece of equipment, risk analysts must cope with other unknowns: if a chemical tank leaks, one cannot determine beforehand the exact amount of pollutant released, the precise shape of the resulting dose-response curves for people exposed, or the values of the rate constants governing the chemical reactions that convert the contents of the tank to more or less dangerous forms. Such uncertainties are often repre-sented by means of probability distributions, which describe the odds that a quantity will take on a specific value within a range of possible levels.

When risk specialists must estimate the likelihood that a part will fail or assign a range of uncertainty to an essential value in a model, they can sometimes use data collected from similar systems elsewhere— although the design of a proposed chemical plant as a whole may be new, the components in its high-pressure steam systems will basically be indistinguishable from those in other plants.

In other cases, however, historical data are not available. Sometimes workers can build predictive models to estimate probabilities based on what is known about roughly similar systems, but often they must rely on expert subjective judgment. Because of the way people think about uncertainty, this approach may involve serious biases. Even so, quantitative risk analysis retains the advantage that judgments can be incorporated in a way that makes assumptions and biases explicit.

Only a few years ago such detailed study of risks required months of custom programming and days or weeks of mainframe computer time. Today a variety of powerful, general-purpose tools are available to make calculations involving uncertainty. These programs, many of which run on personal computers, are revolutionizing the field. They enable accomplished analysts to complete projects that just a decade ago were considered beyond the reach of all but the most sophisticated organizations [*see box on page 40*]. Although using such software requires training, they could democratize risk assessment and make rigorous determinations far more widely available.

After they have determined the likelihood that a system could expose people to harm and described the particulars of the damage that could result from exposure, some risk analysts believe their job is almost done. In fact, they have just completed the preliminaries. Once a risk has been identified and analyzed, psychological and social processes of perception and valuation come into play. How people view and evaluate particular

Risk Analysis in Action

Uncertainty is a central element of most problems involving risk. Analysts today have a number of software tools that incorporate the effects of uncertainty. These tools can show the logical consequences of a particular set of risk assumptions and rules for making decisions about it. One such system is Demos, developed by Max Henrion of Lumina Decision Systems in Palo Alto, Calif.

To see how the process works, consider a hypothetical chemical pollutant, "TXC." To simplify matters, assume that the entire population at risk (30 million people) is exposed to the same dose—this makes a model of exposure processes unnecessary. The next step is to construct a function that describes the risk associated with any given exposure level—for example, a linear dose-response function, possibly with a threshold below which there is no danger.

Given this information, Demos can estimate the number of excess deaths caused every year by TXC exposure. According to the resulting cumulative probability distribution, there is about a 30 percent chance that no one dies, about a 50 percent chance that fewer than 100 people die each year and about a 10 percent chance that more than 1,000 die.

Meanwhile, for a price, pollution controls can reduce the concentration of TXC. (The cost of achieving any given reduction, like the danger of exposure, is determined by consultation with experts.) To choose a level of pollution control that minimizes total social costs, one must first decide how much society is willing to invest to prevent mortality. The upper and lower bounds in this example are $300,000 and $3 million per death averted. (Picking such numbers is a value judgment; in practice, a crucial part of the analysis would be to find out how sensitive the results are to the dollar values placed on life or health.)

Net social costs, in this model, are simply the sum of control costs and mortality. At $300,000 per death averted, their most likely value reaches a minimum when TXC emissions are reduced by 55 percent. At $3 million, the optimum reduction is about 88 percent.

Demos can also calculate a form of correlation between each of the input variables and total costs. Strong correlations indicate variables that contribute significantly to the uncertainty in the final cost estimate. At low levels of pollution control, possible variations in the slope of the damage function, in the location of the threshold and in the base concentration of the pollutant contribute the most to total uncertainty. At very high levels of control, in contrast, almost all the uncertainty derives from unknowns in the cost of controlling emissions.

Finally, Demos can compute the difference in expected cost between the optimal decision based on current information and that given perfect information—that is, the benefit of removing all uncertainties from the calculations. This is known in decision analysis as the

continued on following page

continued from previous page

expected value of perfect information; it is an upper bound on the value of research. If averting a single death is worth $300,000 to society, this value is $38 million a year; if averting a death is worth $3 million, it is $71 million a year.

Although tools such as Demos put quantitative risk analysis within reach of any group with a personal computer, using them properly requires substantial education. My colleagues and I found that a group of first-year engineering doctoral students first exposed to Demos tended to ignore possible correlations among variables, thus seriously over-estimating the uncertainty of their results.

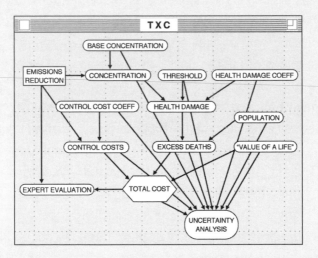

Blocks in the diagram above can be expanded to call up a window containing graphs and tables for their assumptions, equations and probability distributions [when viewing the online article].

risks determines which of the many changes that may occur in the world they choose to notice and perhaps do something about. Someone must then establish the rules for weighing risks, for deciding if the risk is to be controlled and, if so, how. Risk management thus tends to force a society to consider what it cares about and who should bear the burden of living with or mitigating a problem once it has been identified.

For many years, most economists and technologists perceived risk simply in terms of expected value. Working for a few hours in a coal mine, eating peanut butter sandwiches every day for a month, and living next to a nuclear power plant for five years all involve an increased risk of death of about one in a million, so analysts viewed them all as equally risky. When people are asked to rank various activities and technologies in terms of risk, however, they produce lists whose order does not correspond very closely to the number of expected deaths. As a result, some early risk analysts decided that people were confused and that their opinions should be discounted.

Since then, social scientists have conducted extensive studies of public risk perception and discovered that the situation is considerably more subtle. When people are asked to order well-known hazards in terms of the number of deaths and injuries they cause every year, on average they can do it pretty well. If, however, they are asked to rank those hazards in terms of risk, they produce quite a different order.

People do not define risk solely as the expected number of deaths or injuries per unit time. Experimental psychologists Baruch Fischhoff of Carnegie Mellon University and Paul Slovic and Sarah Lichtenstein of Decision Research in Eugene, Ore., have shown that people also rank risks based on how well the process in question is understood, how equitably the danger is distributed, how well individuals can control their exposure and whether risk is assumed voluntarily.

Slovic and his colleagues have found that these factors can be combined into three major groups. The first is basically an event's degree of dreadfulness (as determined by such features as the scale of its effects and the degree to which it affects "innocent" bystanders). The second is a measure of how well the risk is understood, and the third is the number of people exposed. These groups of characteristics can be used to define a "risk space." Where a hazard falls within this space says quite a lot about how people are likely to respond to it. Risks carrying a high level of "dread," for example, provoke more calls for government intervention than do some more workaday risks that actually cause more deaths or injuries.

In making judgments about uncertainty, including ones about risk, experimental psychologists have found that people unconsciously use a number of heuristics. Usually these rules of thumb work well, but under some circumstances they can lead to systematic bias or other errors. As a result, people tend to underestimate the frequency of very common causes of death—stroke, cancer, accidents—by roughly a factor of 10. They also overestimate the frequency of very uncommon causes of death (botulism poisoning, for example) by as much as several orders of magnitude.

These mistakes apparently result from the so-called heuristic of availability. Daniel Kahneman of the University of California at Berkeley, Amos N. Tversky of Stanford University and others have found that people often judge the likelihood of an event in terms of how easily they can recall (or imagine) examples. In this case, stroke is a very common cause of death, but most people learn about it only when a close friend or relative or famous person dies; in contrast, virtually every time someone dies of botulism, people are likely to hear about it on the evening news. This heuristic and others are not limited to the general public. Even experts sometimes employ them in making judgments about uncertainty.

Once people have noticed a risk and decided that they care enough to do something about it, just what should they do? How should they decide the amount to be spent on reducing the risk, and on whom should they place the primary burdens? Risk managers can intervene at many points: they can work to prevent the process producing the risk, to reduce exposures, to modify effects, to alter perceptions or valuations through education and public relations or to compensate for damage after the fact. Which strategy is best depends in large part on the attributes of the particular risk.

Even before determining how to intervene, risk managers must choose the rules that will be used to judge whether to deal with a particular issue and, if so, how much attention, effort and money to devote. Most rules fall into one of three broad classes: utility based, rights based and technology based. The first kind of rules attempt to maximize net benefits. Analysts add up the pros and cons of a particular course of action and take the difference between the two. The course with the best score wins.

Early benefit-cost analyses employed fixed estimates of the value of good and bad outcomes. Many workers now use probabilistic estimates instead to reflect the inherent uncertainty of their descriptions. Although decisions are ultimately made in terms of expected values, other measures may be employed as well. For example, if the principal concern is to avoid disasters, analysts could adopt a "minimax" criterion, which seeks to minimize the harm done by the worst possible outcome, even if that leads to worse results on average.

Of course, many tricky points are involved in such calculations. Costs and benefits may not depend linearly on the amount of pollutant emitted or on the number of dollars spent for control. Furthermore, not all the pros and cons of an issue can necessarily be measured on the same scale. When the absolute magnitude of net benefits cannot be estimated, however, rules based on relative criteria such as cost-effectiveness can still aid decision makers.

Rights-based rules replace the notion of utility with one of justice. In most utility-based systems, anything can be subject to trade-offs; in rights-based ones, however, there are certain things that one party cannot do to another without its consent, regardless of costs or benefits. This is the approach that Congress has taken (at least formally) in the Clean Air Act of 1970: the law does not call for maximizing net social benefit; instead it just requires controlling pollutant concentrations so as to protect the most sensitive populations exposed to them. The underlying presumption holds that these individuals have a right to protection from harm.

Technology-based criteria, in contrast to the first two types, are not concerned with costs, benefits or rights but rather with the level of technology available to control certain risks. Regulations based on these criteria typically mandate "the best available technology" or emissions that are "as low as reasonably achievable." Such rules can be difficult to apply because people seldom agree on the definitions of "available" or "reasonably achievable." Furthermore, technological advances may impose an unintended moving target on both regulators and industry.

There is no correct choice among the various criteria for making decisions about risks. They depend on the ethical and value preferences of individuals and society at large. It is, however, critically important that decision frameworks be carefully and explicitly chosen and that these choices be kept logically consistent, especially in complex situations. To do otherwise may produce inconsistent approaches to the same risk. The EPA has slipped into this error by writing different rules to govern exposure to sources of radioactivity that pose essentially similar risks.

Implicit in the process of risk analysis and management is the crucial role of communication. If public bodies are to make good decisions about regulating potential hazards, citizens must be well informed. The alternative of entrusting policy to panels of experts working behind closed doors has proved a failure, both because the resulting policy may ignore important social considerations and because it may prove impossible to implement in the face of grass-roots resistance.

Until the mid-1980s, there was little research on communicating risks to the public. Over the past five years, along with my colleagues Fischhoff and Lester B. Lave, I have found that much of the conventional wisdom in this area does not hold up. The chemical industry, for example, distilled years of literature about communication into advice for plant managers on ways to make public comparisons between different kinds of risks. We subjected the advice to empirical evaluation and found that it is wrong. We have concluded that the only way to communicate risks reliably is to start by learning what people already know and what they need to know, then develop messages, test them and refine them until surveys demonstrate that the messages have conveyed the intended information.

In 1989 we looked at the effects of the EPA's general brochure about radon in homes. The EPA prepared this brochure according to traditional methods: ask scientific experts what they think people should be told and then package the result in an attractive form. In fact, people are rarely completely ignorant about a risk, and so they filter any message through their existing knowledge. A message that does not take this filtering process into account can be ignored or misinterpreted.

To study people's mental models, we began with a set of open-ended interviews, first asking, "Tell me about radon." Our questions grew more specific only in the later stages of the interview. The number of new ideas encountered in such interviews approached an asymptotic limit after a couple of dozen people. At this point, we devised a closed-form questionnaire from the results of the interviews and administered it to a much larger sample.

We uncovered critical misunderstandings in beliefs that could undermine the effectiveness of the EPA's messages. For example, a sizable proportion of the public believes that radon contamination is permanent and does not go away. This misconception presumably results from an inappropriate inference based on knowledge about chemical contaminants or long-lived radioisotopes. The first version of the EPA's "Citizen's Guide to Radon" did not discuss this issue. Based in part on our findings, the latest version addresses it explicitly.

The objective of risk communication is to provide people with a basis for making an informed decision; any effective message must contain information that helps them in that task. With former doctoral students Ann Bostrom, now at the Georgia Institute of Technology, and Cynthia J. Atman, now at the University of Pittsburgh, we used our method to develop two brochures about radon and compared their effectiveness with that of the EPA's first version. When we asked people to recall simple facts, they did equally well with all three brochures. But when faced with tasks that required inference—advising a neighbor with a high radon reading on what to do— people who received our literature dramatically outperformed those who received the EPA material.

We have found similar misperceptions in other areas, say, climatic change. Only a relatively small proportion of people associate energy use and carbon dioxide emissions with global warming. Many believe the hole in the ozone layer is the factor most likely to lead to global warming, although in fact the two issues are only loosely connected. Some also think launches of spacecraft are the major contributor to holes in the ozone layer. (Willett Kempton of the University of Delaware has found very similar perceptions.)

The essence of good risk communication is very simple: learn what people already believe, tailor the communication to this knowledge and to the decisions people face and then subject the resulting message to careful empirical evaluation. Yet almost no one communicates risks to the public in this fashion. People get their information in fragmentary bits through a press that often does not understand technical details and often chooses to emphasize the sensational. Those trying to convey information are generally either advocates promoting a particular agenda or regulators who sometimes fail either to do their homework or to take a sufficiently broad perspective on the risks they manage. The surprise is not that opinion on hazards may undergo wide swings or may sometimes force silly or inefficient outcomes. It is that the public does as well as it does.

Indeed, when people are given balanced information and enough time to reflect on it, they can do a remarkably good job of deciding what problems are important and of systematically addressing decisions about risks. I conducted studies with Gordon Hester (then a doctoral student, now at the Electric Power Research Institute) in which we asked opinion leaders— a teacher, a state highway patrolman, a bank manager and so on—to play the role of a citizens' board advising the governor of Pennsylvania on the siting of high-voltage electric transmission lines. We asked the groups to focus particularly on the controversial problem of health risks from electric and magnetic fields emanating from transmission lines. We gave them detailed background information and a list of specific questions. Working mostly on their own, over a period of about a day and a half (with pay), the groups structured policy problems and prepared advice in a fashion that would be a credit to many consulting firms.

If anyone should be faulted for the poor quality of responses to risk, it is probably not the public but rather risk managers in government and industry. First, regulators have generally adopted a short-term perspective focused on taking action quickly rather than investing in the research needed to improve understanding of particular hazards in the future. This focus is especially evident in regulations that have been formulated to ensure the safety of the environment, workplace and consumer products.

Second, these officials have often adopted too narrow an outlook on the risks they manage. Sometimes attempts to reduce one risk (burns from flammable children's pajamas) have created others (the increased chance of cancer from fireproofing chemicals).

In some instances, regulators have ignored large risks while attacking smaller ones with vigor. Biologist Bruce Ames of Berkeley has argued persuasively that government risk managers have invested enormous resources in controlling selected artificial carcinogens while ignoring natural ones that may contribute far more to the total risk for human cancer.

Third, government risk managers do not generally set up institutions for learning from experience. Too often adversarial procedures mix attempts to figure out what has happened in an incident with the assignment of blame. As a result, valuable safety-related insights may either be missed or sealed away from the public eye. Civilian aviation, in contrast, has benefited extensively from accident investigations by the National Transportation Safety Board. The board does its work in isolation from arguments about liability; its results are widely published and have contributed measurably to improving air safety.

Many regulators are probably also too quick to look for single global solutions to risk problems. Experimenting with multiple solutions to see which ones work best is a strategy that deserves far more attention than it has received. With 50 states in a federal system, the U.S. has a natural opportunity to run such experiments.

Finally, risk managers have not been sufficiently inventive in developing arrangements that permit citizens to become involved in decision making in a significant and constructive way, working with experts and with adequate time and access to information. Although there are provisions for public hearings in the licensing process for nuclear reactors or the siting of hazardous waste repositories, the process rarely allows for reasoned discussion, and input usually comes too late to have any effect on the set of alternatives under consideration.

Thomas Jefferson was right: the best strategy for assuring the general welfare in a democracy is a well-informed electorate. If the U.S. and other nations want better, more reasoned social decisions about risk, they need to take steps to enhance public understanding. They must also provide institutions whereby citizens and their representatives can devote attention to risk management decisions. This will not preclude the occasional absurd outcome, but neither does any other way of making decisions. Moreover, appropriate public involvement should go a long way toward eliminating the confrontational tone that has become so common in the risk management process.

The Author

M. Granger Morgan has worked for many years to improve techniques for analyzing and managing risks to health, safety and the environment. Morgan heads the department of engineering and public policy at Carnegie Mellon University. He also holds appointments in the department of electrical and computer engineering and at the H. John Heinz III School of Public Policy and Management. Morgan received a B.A. from Harvard University, an M.S. from Cornell University and a Ph.D. in applied physics from the University of California, San Diego.

In this second look at risk analysis and management, the authors (one is an economist, another is a physicist, and the third is a computer scientist) describe an approach they say is better than traditional methods for making long-range decisions. They say it allows them to turn the usual question of "What will the future bring?" into one they feel better reflects our real concern, namely, "What actions today will best shape the future to our liking?" Rather than look for the best (optimal) answer, which is bound to fail when any of its sharply tuned assumptions fail, they look at a large number of robust, "good enough" scenarios that cover a wide range of possibilities. These robust scenarios yield satisfactory outcomes in "easy-to-envision futures," as well as in "hard-to-anticipate contingencies." The approach is also poised to jump to another scenario if more information comes in and indicates this should happen.

Also, traditional approaches for making long-range decisions "gravitate to the well-understood parts of the challenge" and tend to overlook the value of the rest. In contrast, the authors say, their approach highlights uncertainty and tries to find ways to manage it. This allows decision makers to explore a "rich variety of what-if scenarios," and provides a way to "break the ideological logjam that too often arises in Washington, D.C." —RA

"Shaping the Future"
by Steven W. Popper, Robert J. Lempert, and
Steven C. Bankes
Scientific American, April 2005

Last year a high-profile panel of experts known as
the Copenhagen Consensus ranked the world's most
pressing environmental, health and social problems in a
prioritized list. Assembled by the Danish Environmental
Assessment Institute under its then director, Bjørn
Lomborg, the panel used cost-benefit analysis to evaluate
where a limited amount of money would do the most
good. It concluded that the highest priority should go
to immediate concerns with relatively well understood
cures, such as control of malaria. Long-term challenges
such as climate change, where the path forward and even
the scope of the threat remain unclear, ranked lower.

Usually each of these problems is treated in isolation,
as though humanity had the luxury of dealing with its
problems one by one. The Copenhagen Consensus used
state-of-the-art techniques to try to bring a broader
perspective. In so doing, however, it revealed how the
state of the art fails to grapple with a simple fact: the
future is uncertain. Attempts to predict it have a
checkered history—from declarations that humans
would never fly, to the doom-and-gloom economic and
environmental forecasts of the 1970s, to claims that
the "New Economy" would do away with economic
ups and downs. Not surprisingly, those who make
decisions tend to stay focused on the next fiscal quarter,

the next year, the next election. Feeling unsure of their compass, they hug the familiar shore.

This understandable response to an uncertain future means, however, that the nation's and the world's long-term threats often get ignored altogether or are even made worse by shortsighted decisions. In everyday life, responsible people look out for the long term despite the needs of the here and now: we do homework, we save for retirement, we take out insurance. The same principles should surely apply to society as a whole. But how can leaders weigh the present against the future? How can they avoid being paralyzed by scientific uncertainty?

In well-understood situations, science can reliably predict the implications of alternative policy choices. These predictions, combined with formal methods of decision analysis that use mathematical models and statistical methods to determine optimal courses of action, can specify the trade-offs that society must inevitably make. Corporate executives and elected officials may not always heed this advice, but they do so more often than a cynic might suppose. Analysis has done much to improve the quality of lawmaking, regulation and investment. National economic policy is one example. Concepts introduced by analysts in the 1930s and 1940s—unemployment rate, current-account deficit and gross national product—are now commonplace. For the most part, governments have learned to avoid the radical boom-and-bust cycles that were common in the 19th and early 20th centuries.

The trouble now is that the world faces a number of challenges, both long- and short-term, that are far from well understood: how to preserve the environment, ensure the future of Social Security, guard against terrorism and manage the effects of novel technology. These problems are simply too complex and contingent for scientists to make definitive predictions. In the presence of such deep uncertainty, the machinery of prediction and decision making seizes up. Traditional analytical approaches gravitate to the well-understood parts of the challenge and shy away from the rest. Hence, even sophisticated analyses such as the one by the Copenhagen Consensus have trouble assessing the value of near-term steps that might shape our long-term future.

The three of us—an economist, a physicist and a computer scientist all working in RAND's Pardee Center—have been fundamentally rethinking the role of analysis. We have constructed rigorous, systematic methods for dealing with deep uncertainty. The basic idea is to liberate ourselves from the need for precise prediction by using the computer to help frame strategies that work well over a very wide range of plausible futures. Rather than seeking to eliminate uncertainty, we highlight it and then find ways to manage it. Already companies such as Volvo have used our techniques to plan corporate strategy.

The methods offer a way to break the ideological logjam that too often arises in Washington, D.C. By allowing decision makers to explore a rich variety of

Overview/*Dealing with Uncertainty*

- Science has become an essential part of decision making by governments and businesses, but uncertainty can foil decision-making frameworks such as cost-benefit analysis. People often end up doing nothing or taking steps that worsen the long-term outlook.
- The authors have developed an alternative framework focused on flexibility—finding, testing and implementing policies that work well no matter what happens.
- Policies can have built-in mechanisms to change with the circumstances. For climate change, one such mechanism is a "safety valve" to ensure that emissions reductions occur but do not get too expensive.

what-if scenarios, the new approach reframes the age-old but unanswerable question—What will the long-term future bring?—to one better reflecting our real concern: What actions today will best shape the future to our liking?

The Perils of Prediction

Striking a balance between the economy and the environment is one leading example of the difficulty in using science to inform long-term decisions. In his 2002 book *The Future of Life*, Edward O. Wilson described the debate between economists and environmental scientists [see "The Bottleneck," by Edward O. Wilson; SCIENTIFIC AMERICAN, February 2002]. The former group frequently argues that present policies will guide society successfully through the coming century. Technological innovation will reduce pollution and improve energy efficiency, and changes in commodity prices will ensure timely switching from scarce to more plentiful resources. The latter group argues that society's present course will prove unsustainable. By the time the signs of environmental stress become unambiguous, society may have passed the point of easy recovery. Better to apply the brakes now rather than jam them on later when it may be too late.

No matter how compelling their arguments, both sides' detailed predictions are surely wrong. Decisions made today will affect the world 50 to 100 years hence, but no one can credibly predict what life will be like then, regardless of the quality of the science. Interested parties view the same incomplete data, apply different values and assumptions, and arrive at different conclusions. The result can be static and acrimonious debate: "Tree hugger!" "Eco-criminal!"

The (in)famous report *The Limits to Growth* from the early 1970s is the perfect example of how the standard tools of analysis often fail to mediate such debates. A group of scientists and opinion leaders called the Club of Rome predicted that the world would soon exhaust its natural resources unless it took immediate action to slow their use. This conclusion flowed from a then state-of-the-art computer model of the dynamics of resource use. The report met with great skepticism. Since the days of Thomas Malthus, impending resource shortages have melted away as new technologies have made production more efficient and provided alternatives to dwindling resources.

But the model was not wrong; it was just used incorrectly. Any computer model is, by definition, a simplified mirror of the real world, its predictions vulnerable to some neglected factor. The model developed for *The Limits to Growth* revealed some important aspects of the challenges faced by society. In presenting the analysis as a forecast, the authors stretched the model beyond its limits and reduced the credibility of their entire research program.

Grappling with the Future

Conscious of this failing, analysts have turned to techniques such as scenario planning that involve exploring different possible futures rather than gambling on a single prediction. As an example, in 1995 the Global Scenario Group, convened by the Stockholm Environment Institutes, developed three scenario families. The "Conventional Worlds" family described a future in which technological innovation, driven by markets and lightly steered by government policy, produces economic growth without undermining environmental quality. In the "Barbarization" set of scenarios, the same factors—innovation, markets and policy—prove inadequate to the challenge, leading to social collapse and the spread of violence and misery. The third set, "Great Transitions," portrayed the widespread adoption of eco-friendly social values. The Global Scenario Group argued that the Conventional Worlds scenarios are plausible but not guaranteed; to avoid the risk of Barbarization, society should follow the Great Transitions paths.

Although scenario analysis avoids making definite predictions, it has its own shortcomings. It addresses no more than a handful of the many plausible futures, so skeptics can always question the choice of the highlighted few. More fundamentally, scenario families do not translate easily into plans for action. How should decision makers use the scenarios? Should they focus on the most threatening case or the one regarded by experts as most likely? Each approach has faults.

The European Union often favors the "precaution-ary principle"—in essence, basing policy on the most hazardous plausible scenarios. The Kyoto treaty on climate change, for example, requires reductions of greenhouse gas emissions even though their long-term effects are far from understood. On one level, the precautionary principle makes perfect sense. It is better to be safe than sorry. The long-term future will always be cloudy; some dangers may become certain only when it is too late to prevent them. Yet the principle is an imperfect guide. The future presents many potential harms. Should we worry about them all equally? Few choices are risk-free, and the precautionary principle can lead to contradictory conclusions. For instance, both the harm from greenhouse gas emissions and the cost of reducing them are uncertain. To safeguard the environment, we should reduce the emissions now. To safeguard the economy, we should postpone reductions. So what do we do?

In contrast, many in the U.S. favor cost-benefit analysis, which balances the benefits of eliminating each potential harm against the costs of doing so. When outcomes are uncertain, cost-benefit analysis weights them with odds. We should be willing to pay up to $500 to eliminate a $1,000 harm whose chance of occurring is 50–50. Cost-benefit analysis provides unambiguous answers in many instances. Lead in gasoline enters the environment and affects the developing brains of children. Even though scientists do not know precisely how many children are affected, the benefit of removing lead from gasoline far exceeds the cost. But the long-term future rarely offers such clear choices. Often both the costs and benefits are sufficiently unclear that small disagreements over assigning odds can make a huge difference in the recommended policy.

Making Policies Robust

Traditional tools such as cost-benefit analysis rely on a "predict then act" paradigm. They require a prediction of the future before they can determine the policy that will work best under the expected circumstances. Because these analyses demand that everyone agree on the models and assumptions, they cannot resolve many of the most crucial debates that our society faces. They force people to select one among many plausible, competing views of the future. Whichever choice emerges is vulnerable to blunders and surprises.

Our approach is to look not for optimal strategies but for robust ones. A robust strategy performs well when compared with the alternatives across a wide range of plausible futures. It need not be the optimal strategy in any future; it will, however, yield satisfactory outcomes in both easy-to-envision futures and hard-to-anticipate contingencies.

This approach replicates the way people often reason about complicated and uncertain decisions in everyday life. The late Herbert A. Simon, a cognitive scientist and Nobel laureate who pioneered in the 1950s the study of how people make real-world decisions, observed that they seldom optimize. Rather they seek strategies that will work well enough, that include hedges against various potential outcomes and that are adaptive. Tomorrow will bring information unavailable today; therefore, people plan on revising their plans.

Incorporating robustness and adaptability into formal decision analysis used to be impossible because of the complexity and vast number of required calculations. Technology has overcome these hurdles. Confronting deep uncertainty requires more than raw computational power, though. The computers have to be used differently. Traditional predict-then-act methods treat the computer as a glorified calculator.

Analysts select the model and specify the assumptions; the computer then calculates the optimal strategy implied by these inputs.

In contrast, for robust decision making the computer is integral to the reasoning process. It stress-tests candidate strategies, searching for plausible scenarios that could defeat them. Robust decision making interactively combines the complementary abilities of humans and machines. People excel at seeking patterns, drawing inferences and framing new questions. But they can fail to recognize inconvenient facts and can lose track of how long chains of causes relate to effects. The machine ensures that all claims about strategies are consistent with the data and can reveal scenarios that challenge people's cherished assumptions. No strategy is completely immune to uncertainty, but the computer helps decision makers exploit whatever information they do have to make choices that can endure a wide range of trends and surprises.

Sustainable Development

To see how this approach works in practice, return to the dilemma of sustainable development. The first step is to figure out what exactly the computer should calculate. Robust decision making requires the machine to generate multiple paths into the future, spanning the full diversity of those that might occur. We may not know the exact future that will transpire, but any strategy that performs well across a sufficiently diverse set of computer-generated scenarios is likely to meet the challenges presented by what actually comes to pass.

In our analysis of sustainable development, we used a revised version of the Wonderland model originally created by economist Warren C. Sanderson of Stony Brook University and the International Institute for Applied Systems Analysis in Laxenburg, Austria. The Wonderland simulation incorporates, in a very simple manner, scientific understanding of the dynamics of the global economy, demographics and environment. Growing population and wealth will increase pollution, whereas technological innovation may reduce it. The pollution, in turn, hurts the economy when it taxes the environment beyond its absorptive capacity.

Our version of Wonderland is similar to—but with only 41 uncertain parameters, much simpler than— the simulation used for *The Limits to Growth*. This simplicity can be a virtue: experience demonstrates that additional detail alone does not make predictions more accurate if the model's structure or inputs remain uncertain. For robust planning, models should be used not to predict but to produce a diversity of scenarios, all consistent with the knowledge we do possess.

Running models within special "exploratory modeling" software, analysts can test various strategies and see how they perform. The human user suggests a strategy; for each scenario in the ensemble, the computer compares this approach to the optimal strategy (the one that would have been chosen with perfect predictive foresight) according to such measures as income or life expectancy. A systematic process reveals futures in which the proposed strategies could perform poorly. It also highlights ways each strategy could be adjusted to handle those stressful futures better.

In the sustainability example, we run the model through the year 2100. Two key uncertainties are the average global economic growth rate during this period and the business-as-usual "decoupling rate" (that is, the reduction in pollution per unit of economic output that would occur in the absence of new environmental policies). The decoupling rate will be positive if existing regulations, productivity increases and the shift to a service economy lessen pollution without lessening growth. It can go negative if growth requires an increase in pollution.

Depending on the values of these quantities, different strategies perform differently. One strategy, "Stay the Course," simply continues present policy. It performs well in futures where the decoupling rate exceeds the growth rate, but if the reverse is true, pollution eventually becomes so serious that policy-makers are forced to abandon the strategy and try to reverse the damage. During the 20th century, the growth and decoupling rates were nearly equal. If the same proves to be true for the 21st, the world will totter on a knife-edge between success and failure [*see box on page 68*].

Balancing the Economy and the Environment

How can we clean the planet over the coming century without breaking the bank? The answer depends on how fast the economy will grow and how much existing trends and regulations will cut pollution—and nobody knows either of those things. Many proposed approaches (*below and facing top*) would strike a good balance for some growth rates but not for others, whereas a flexible strategy (*facing bottom*) could handle a wide range of scenarios. In the graphs below, colored boxes correspond to particular future rates of growth and "decoupling" (the pace at which existing trends cut pollution). The colors represent how the strategy compares with the theoretically optimal strategy for each scenario: perfectly (■), acceptably (■), poorly ( ), or very poorly (■). Dots represent historical rates, which may provide some clue for what is to come.

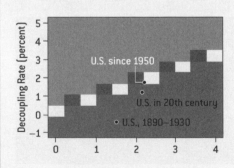

Stay the Course adds no new environmental policies. It is a good approach if the decoupling rate is high; otherwise, a poor one.

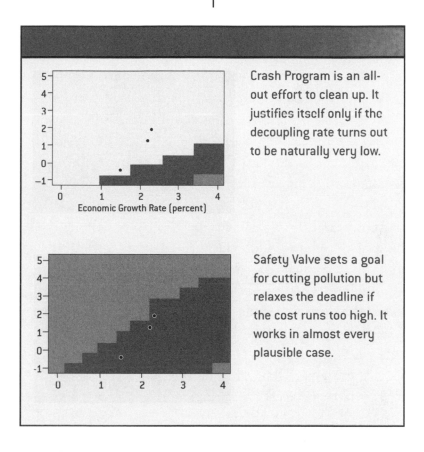

Crash Program is an all-out effort to clean up. It justifies itself only if the decoupling rate turns out to be naturally very low.

Safety Valve sets a goal for cutting pollution but relaxes the deadline if the cost runs too high. It works in almost every plausible case.

The more aggressive "Crash Program" pours money into technological development and environmental regulations that speed decoupling beyond its business-as-usual rate. Although this strategy eliminates the risk of catastrophe, it can impose unnecessarily high costs, inhibiting economic growth.

Becoming Flexible

Both these strategies involve policies that are fixed in advance. An adaptive strategy bests them both. Inspired by the complementary strengths and weaknesses of "Stay the Course" and "Crash Program," we considered a flexible alternative that imposes rigorous emissions limits but relaxes them if they cost too much. Such a strategy can be robust. If the technological optimists are right (the decoupling rate turns out to be high), the cost threshold is never breached and industry meets the aggressive environmental goals. If technological pessimists prove correct (the decoupling rate is low), then tight pollution restrictions will exceed the agreed-on cost limits, in which case the strategy gives industry more time to meet the goals.

Such strategies can help cut through contentious debates by providing plans of action that all can agree will play out no matter whose view of the future proves correct. Our adaptive strategy is similar to the "safety valve" strategies that some economists have proposed as alternatives to the immutable emissions targets in the Kyoto treaty. Our new analytical machinery enables decision makers both to design such strategies and to demonstrate their effectiveness to the various interest groups involved.

Of course, even adaptive strategies have their Achilles' heel. In the case of the safety valve, the combination of environmental goals and cost constraints that works best in most futures performs poorly when technological innovation proves to be extremely expensive. To get around this problem, the user can repeat the analysis to come up with a variety of robust strategies, each of which breaks down under different conditions. One strategy may work well when another fails, and vice versa, so the choice between them involves an unavoidable trade-off. The computer calculates how likely each set of circumstances would have to be to justify picking one strategy over the other. Our method thus reduces a complex problem to a small number of simple choices. Decision makers make the final call. Instead of fruitlessly debating models and other assumptions, they can focus on the fundamental trade-offs, fully aware of the surprises that the future may bring.

Clearly, this approach is applicable not only to sustainable development but also to a wide range of other challenges: bringing new products to market, managing the nation's entitlement programs, even defeating terrorism. Science and technology cannot change the future's fundamental unpredictability. Instead they offer an answer to a different question: Which actions today can best usher in a desirable future? Humans and computers search for plausible futures in which a proposed strategy could fail and then identify means to avoid these potential adverse outcomes.

Past failures of prediction should humble anyone who claims to see a clear course into the decades ahead. Paradoxically, though, our greatest possible influence in shaping the future may extend precisely over those timescales where our gaze becomes most dim. We often have little effect on a predictable, near-term future subject to well-understood forces. Where the future is ill defined, unpredictable and hardest to see, our actions today may well have their most profound effects. New tools can help us chart the right course.

The Authors

Steven W. Popper, Robert J. Lempert and Steven C. Bankes straddle the worlds of science and policymaking. They work at the RAND Corporation in Santa Monica, Calif., one of the country's most renowned think tanks. Popper, an economist, studies how organizations incorporate techno-logical innovation. Lempert, a physicist, specializes in environmental and energy policy. Bankes, a computer scientist, is the father of new methods for computer simu-lations. All have worked with government and international organizations such as the White House Office of Science and Technology Policy, the Department of Defense, the National Science Foundation and the United Nations. They teach in the Pardee RAND Graduate School and are founders of Evolving Logic, a firm developing software to facilitate the robust decision methods discussed in this article.

2 | Domestic Troubles

The 1989 Exxon Valdez *oil spill in Alaska's Prince William Sound was the most damaging oil spill in U.S. history. The 11-million-gallon (41,639,530-liter) spill impacted 1,900 miles (3,058 kilometers) of coastline and caused substantial numbers of wildlife deaths.*

In addition to prompting passage of the Oil Pollution Act of 1990, which required the U.S. Coast Guard to strengthen its regulations on oil tank vessels and banned the Exxon Valdez *from Alaskan waters, the litigation against the Exxon Shipping Company marked the first quantitative application of the contingent valuation method. This method estimated the value of the sound in its pristine state, called its existence value, at about $3 billion. This amount was significantly higher than the value of more tangible losses, such as the losses suffered by fishers, and strengthened the case for more extensive cleanup and follow-up research, according to Jay Johnson, a Southeastern Louisiana University researcher. It also helped make the case that the restoration costs were not excessive. The following article* *describes the suits brought against Exxon, some settled and some ongoing, and the suppressive effect litigation had on the exchange of scientific data on the spill. —RA*

"Sound Science?"
by Marguerite Holloway
Scientific American, August 1993

The 1989 *Exxon Valdez* oil spill seems to have sullied more than the waters and wilderness of Prince William Sound. Because of lawsuits against the petroleum company, many studies about the condition of the ecosystem and wildlife were kept secret until this year. But even now, after the release of findings by Exxon and by the government, no consensus has been reached on what happened to the sound after the 10.8-million-gallon spill and whether it is or is not recovering.

Frustrated researchers say spin has subsumed science. "I find it very disturbing," comments Robert B. Spies, chief scientist for the trustees, a group of federal and state representatives who have overseen damage assessment studies. Investigators "come to opposite conclusions, and then the public asks, 'What good is science if the answer depends on where you are getting your money?'"

Scientists for all parties initially assumed they would share data and then make their own interpretations. Once lawsuits were initiated, however, Exxon and the government trustees banned the release of any information. Open discussion, debate and peer review were suspended. Many scientists continue to worry that the opportunity to learn from the spill was squandered because lawyers shaped the choice of studies. Some decisions about cleanup were also made without relevant data on, for instance, fish populations.

After the 1991 settlement—in which Exxon agreed to pay $1.1 billion to the state and federal governments—the long-awaited data promised to surface. Most of them finally did this past February in Anchorage. Researchers for the trustees presented their findings, cataloguing extensive and, in some cases, ongoing damage to many species of birds, fish and mammals. Although scientists from Exxon were invited to present their work at the same time, they declined.

In late April, Exxon responded with its own meeting in Atlanta. There experts offered a diametrically different view of the sound. They reported that the area was in fact entirely recovered and that contamination had been extensive before the spill. That assertion was based on studies of hydrocarbon fingerprinting, a means of characterizing the source of the oil. Exxon chemists say that before the spill the sound was already polluted by diesel oil and oil from a natural seep. They maintain that federal scientists mistakenly identified oil from these sources as *Exxon Valdez* oil.

"Exxon seems to want to make the claim that there was significant widespread contamination prior to the spill. We don't agree," says Jeffrey W. Short, a chemist at the National Oceanic and Atmospheric Administration (NOAA). "We did a four-year baseline study when the [shipping] terminal opened in 1977. In the course of that study of intertidal sediment, we didn't see any evidence of seep oil and precious little of diesel oil."

Exxon's conclusions about the intertidal region also differ from those of NOAA. Jonathan P. Houghton, a marine biologist who has studied the sound for both Exxon and NOAA, has reported that washing the beaches with hot water was often detrimental and that recovery of the flora and fauna has been slow in some places because of the cleanup. Using an alternative methodology and a different definition of an oiled beach, Exxon scientists reached another conclusion. "We feel, in general, the sound has essentially recovered," comments Alan Maki, chief scientist for Exxon.

It is unlikely that anything more conclusive than a contest of point-counterpoint can emerge from a comparison of the studies for now. The trustees' findings have been peer-reviewed and are currently available to the public. But the company itself has generally released only summaries of its data, and as of yet none of them has been vetted. Exxon faces some $2.6 billion in additional lawsuits brought by Native Americans and fishermen and is not expected to fully reveal its data until after hearings in 1994. In addition, a provision called the "reopener clause" in the 1991 settlement permits the trustees to sue for more money if they discover further damage to the sound.

Many researchers say they cannot wait to get their hands on the data base and sort through the varied interpretations. "I will do it on my own time," Spies exclaims. "I want to see what the scientific basis of all this is." He adds that his concern extends to both groups of researchers. A study by the trustees of abnormality in juvenile herring, for example, concluded that the population at large was affected. "But the data don't really support that yet. It is in a gray area," Spies cautions. On the other hand, given the same data, "Exxon scientists extrapolate that there wasn't an effect."

Despite concerns that have emerged about conducting science during a legal battle, another oil spill would probably give rise to a similar situation. Some experts have advocated establishing independent commissions in such cases. But the precedents are not entirely reassuring, notes Charles H. Peterson, professor of marine science at the University of North Carolina at Chapel Hill. In the 1970s, for instance, environmental organizations sought to block the expansion of the San Onofre nuclear power plant in California.

The utility and the activists agreed to pool funds to study the impact on the environment and to create a review committee—made up of members from industry, conservation groups and academia. Both sides agreed to accept the results. "The concept was good," Peterson says. But after 14 years and $50 million, "the company went off and did its own studies, so it all went to court anyway."

Wetlands hold a special place in environmental policy because their complex, changing nature makes it difficult for proponents to define them in legislation. The authors of the next article explain how an incomplete knowledge of this protean characteristic by policymakers who were considering amendments to the Federal Water Act could have jeopardized a significant number of the wetlands. The measure, House bill 1330, was an attempt to give developers some certainty, and it was ultimately defeated.

These "shallow, water-fed systems" have an important role in reducing pollution, limiting the damaging effects of waves, storing floodwaters, trapping sediment, and providing a source of wild rice, to name a few commercial and utilitarian attributes. They also provide habitat and spawning grounds for a wide range of wildlife. But their constantly changing nature and water levels make it difficult to devise a management program that provides certainty for developers while protecting the wetlands.

"It is not difficult to see how fluctuating water levels and the intricate relations between

wetlands and human development pose serious challenges to any simple wetland policy," the authors write. *"Highly generalized rules are often insensitive to the physical characteristics and dynamics of wetlands." —RA*

"Wetlands"
by Jon A. Kusler, William J. Mitsch, and Joseph S. Larson
Scientific American, January 1994

Variously dry, wet or anywhere between, wetlands are by their nature protean. Such constant change makes wetlands ecologically rich; they are often as diverse as rain forests. These shallow water-fed systems are central to the life cycle of many plants and animals, some of them endangered. They provide a habitat as well as spawning grounds for an extraordinary variety of creatures and nesting areas for migratory birds. Some wetlands even perform a global function. The northern peat lands of Canada, Alaska and Eurasia, in particular, may help moderate climatic change by serving as a sink for the greenhouse gas carbon dioxide.

Wetlands also have commercial and utilitarian functions. They are sources of lucrative harvests of wild rice, furbearing animals, fish and shellfish. Wetlands limit the damaging effects of waves, convey and store floodwaters, trap sediment and reduce pollution—the last attribute has earned them the sobriquet "nature's kidneys."

Despite their value, wetlands are rapidly disappearing. In the U.S., more than half of these regions in every state except Alaska and Hawaii have been destroyed. Between the 1950s and the 1970s more than nine million acres—an area equivalent to the combined size of Massachusetts, Connecticut and Rhode Island—were wiped out. Some states have almost entirely lost their wetlands: California and Ohio, for example, retain only 10 percent of their original expanse. Destruction continues today, albeit at a slightly reduced rate, in part, because there are fewer wetlands to eliminate. No such numbers are available internationally, but we estimate that 6 percent of all land is currently wetlands.

The extensive losses can generally be attributed to the same feature that makes wetlands so valuable: their ever changing nature. The complex dynamics of wetlands complicate efforts to create policies for preserving them. Their management and protection must incorporate a realistic definition, one that encompasses all these intricate swamps to vernal pools, playa lakes and prairie potholes. If scientists can better clarify and communicate to the public and to policymakers the special characteristics of wetlands as well as their economic and ecological importance, perhaps those that do remain will not disappear.

Over the years, researchers and government agencies have developed many definitions of wetlands. All share the recognition that wetlands are shallow-water systems, or areas where water is at or near the surface for some time. Most descriptions also note the presence of plants adapted to flooding, called hydrophytes, and hydric soils, which, when flooded, develop colors and odors that distinguish them from upland soils.

Wetlands can be found in diverse topographical settings. They arise in flat, tidally inundated but protected areas, such as salt marshes and mangrove swamps. Wetlands exist next to freshwater rivers, streams and lakes and their floodplains (such areas are often called riparian). In addition, they form in surface depressions almost anywhere. Such wetlands comprise freshwater marshes, potholes, meadows, playas and vernal pools where vegetation is not woody, as well as swamps where it is. Wetlands can also flourish on slopes and at the base of slopes, supplied by springs, and as bogs and fens fed by precipitation and groundwater. Finally, they can occur in cold climates where permafrost retains water and low evaporation rates prevail.

Although the kinds and locations of wetlands vary greatly, fluctuating water levels are central to all of them. Water rises or falls in accordance with tides, precipitation or runoff; the activities of humans and other animals can also determine water levels. The extent of the fluctuation is often very different from site to site. In the salt marshes of the northeastern U.S. and eastern Canada, daily tides may bring about shifts of 10 feet or more in water level. Other regions undergo even more extreme changes. For example, rainfall can cause the Amazon River to rise 25 feet during a season and invade neighboring wetlands [see "Flooded Forests of the Amazon, " by Michael Goulding; SCIENTIFIC AMERICAN, March 1993]. In the prairie potholes of the Midwest, groundwater or melting snow may alter water levels by four or five feet over several years.

Even when levels fluctuate dramatically, these systems can adjust so that they sustain little permanent damage. Indeed, the very existence of some wetlands is related to the ravages of hurricanes, floods and droughts. Most wetlands along rivers and coastlines as well as those that formed in depressions in the landscape are long-lived precisely because of events that people consider economically devastating. Raging fires burn excess deposited organic matter and recycle nutrients. Hurricanes and high-velocity floods scour sediments and organic matter, removing them from wetlands or creating wetlands nearby. Droughts temporarily destroy hydrophytic vegetation and allow oxidation and compaction of organic soils.

This anomalous feature of wetlands—the way that short-term destruction ensures long-term gain—is poorly understood by the general public. Much of the press coverage of Hurricane Andrew and its impact on the Florida Everglades illustrates this fact. Although the damage was serious, the ecosystem and others like it have survived thousands of such cataclysms. Some researchers have suggested that trees in the coastal mangrove swamps reach maturity at about 30 years of age, a periodicity that coincides almost perfectly with the frequency of hurricanes in the tropics.

Misunderstanding has also led to many well-intentioned proposals to stabilize water levels in wetlands. The flooding along the Mississippi, Missouri and other rivers last summer was especially severe because wetlands had been destroyed as people built on them. These ecosystems could no longer serve to absorb floodwaters.

Of course, the levels of many bodies of water rise and fall. Lakes and streams are occupied by plants and animals that are adapted to a permanently watery environment—even temporary dry spells could kill them. In contrast, a wetland encompasses an array of shallow-water and saturated soil environments that possess some elements of a terrestrial system and some of an aquatic system. Because water levels rise and fall continuously, portions of wetlands—and, in some cases, entire wetlands—at times resemble true aquatic systems, at times terrestrial systems and at times intermediate systems. Plants, animals and microbes are constantly adapting and changing.

Wetlands also differ from deep-water aquatic systems in their sensitivity to the effects of water-level changes. A one-foot change in the level of a lake or a river brings about little difference in a system's boundaries or functions. But an equivalent change in a wetland can significantly affect both. Certain wetland vegetation—sedges, grasses or floating plants—often grows in one location during a wet year, another location during an intermediate year and not at all during a dry year. Thus, cycles of plant growth can change over time.

The Fluctuating Water Levels of Wetlands

Wetlands are often as different in their appearance and in the species they host as they are in the range of saturation they experience in the course of a year or a season. Their topographical variety and the complexity of their hydrology have made some wetlands difficult to identify and, hence, difficult to preserve.

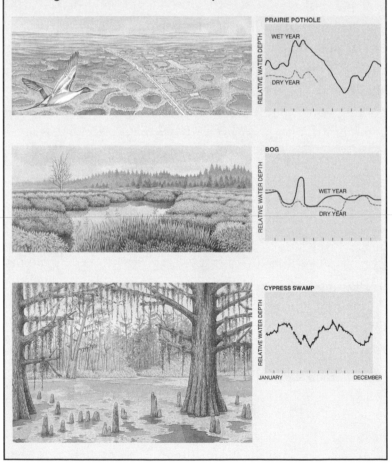

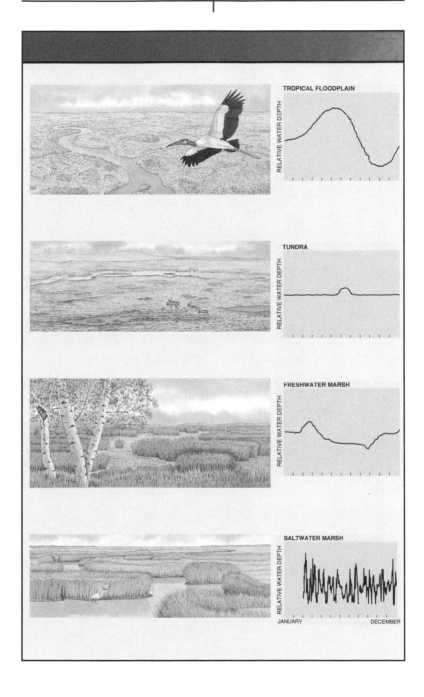

TROPICAL FLOODPLAIN

RELATIVE WATER DEPTH

TUNDRA

RELATIVE WATER DEPTH

FRESHWATER MARSH

RELATIVE WATER DEPTH

SALTWATER MARSH

RELATIVE WATER DEPTH

JANUARY   DECEMBER

As a result, the kinds of animals that frequent a wetland will also vary.

Such shifts explain the immense biodiversity of wetlands. Alterations in their water levels give rise to a series of ecological niches that can support terrestrial, partially aquatic and fully aquatic plants and animals. In addition, vertical gradients caused by differing depths of water and saturation create further environmental variation. Wetlands essentially borrow species from both aquatic and terrestrial realms.

Even a temporary niche can be crucial to the nesting, spawning, breeding or feeding patterns of a particular species. Short-legged birds such as greenbacked herons and limpkins feed along shallow-water shorelines. Longer-legged species, including egrets and great blue herons, feed in deeper water. Swimming waterfowl such as mallards, coots and purple gallinules feed in the deepest open water. Shifts in water levels serve to trigger nesting by wood storks in Florida and breeding by ducks in prairie potholes.

Rising and falling water levels not only influence the internal character of a wetland, but they also link wetlands to one another and to other aquatic systems. Because of their sensitivity to water levels, wetlands are highly dependent on the quantity and quality of water in their immediate area. This fact is particularly true for isolated or small wetlands. In such terrain, rain, local runoff and the aquifer are the only sources of water. Wetlands bordering major lakes and streams

Bottomland hardwood wetlands that occur in the major river basins of the southeastern U.S. have two very distinct hydroperiods, or periods of inundation. During the dry season (*top*), fish species such as the yellow bullhead stay in the channel, whereas animals and birds move throughout all zones of the region. But during the flooded period (*bottom*), the crucial role of the wetland as spawning ground and nursery becomes evident. The fish move into the inundated forest, where they spawn and feed; wood ducks fly into the area to nest. Many other creatures move upland to dry ground. The bottomland hardwood plants and animals are thus adapted to both the dry and wet periods.

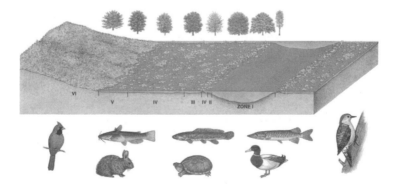

may be less sensitive to such natural changes. They rely on the levels in adjacent water bodies that, in turn, depend on precipitation in larger watersheds. Coastal wetlands are also somewhat more resilient since levels depend on the tides.

Such associations with the neighboring environment are critical to wetland functions. Wetlands can serve as reproductive or feeding sites for some species only if they are connected with other waterways. Moreover, the incoming water brings nutrients and sediments that can make the system more productive. The wetlands then cleanse these waters by retaining sediments as well as phosphorus and other chemicals. Pollutants such as nitrogen can be turned into harmless gases by the aerobic and anaerobic bacteria found there.

Clearly, the dependence of many wetlands on contiguous water systems makes them especially vulnerable to even minor human activity. Development in watershed areas and the pumping of groundwater can disrupt or destroy them. Landfills, dikes or other measures that isolate wetlands from nearby wetlands or waters can reduce their ability to provide flood storage, water purification and habitats.

Barriers also can prevent wetland plants and animals with highly sensitive aquatic tolerances from migrating up and down gentle slopes. Without sufficient room to move, wetlands themselves may temporarily or permanently disappear. Some—including headwater riparian wetlands, depressional wetlands and slope wetlands—

are particularly prone to such interference. A seawall or a dike at the landward boundary of a salt marsh can prevent the inland migration of the marsh when the sea level rises. Indeed, such diking currently threatens, rather than helps, many coastal areas.

Increased amounts of sediment, nutrients and pesticides from watersheds undergoing development can drastically alter the biological makeup of a wetland and overload its ability to purge pollutants if they are added beyond the wetland's ability to assimilate them. Such additions can even destroy a wetland in a short time. Isolated wetlands arising in topological depressions are quite vulnerable because they are not periodically purged of sediment by storms or high-velocity river flows.

Many pothole and kettle-hole wetlands in the northern American states and the southern parts of Canadian provinces are at just such risk. Most wetlands in these regions were created 8,000 to 12,000 years ago by the retreat of the glaciers. As blocks of ice in glacial outwash and till (the assemblage of rocks, boulders and clay that rides along with the glacier) melted, pothole depressions were formed. The deeper ones became lakes; the shallow ones, wetlands. In presettlement times, heavily vegetated surroundings contributed small amounts of sediment and nutrients to these wetlands. But the clearing of land increased this influx of sediment, which continues to build up because the ecosystems lack effective flushing mechanisms.

Ironically, decreased sediment from dams and reservoirs along rivers and streams threatens other wetlands. In the Mississippi Delta, levees have prevented loads of sediment from being deposited—to the point that marshes can no longer build up at a rate equal to sea-level rise and land subsidence. The result is a massive loss, an estimated 25,000 acres of marsh every year. Watershed development and diversions that decrease the freshwater flow of rivers similarly threaten many estuarine wetlands by reducing the quantity of freshwater and increasing salinity.

It is not difficult to see how fluctuating water levels and the intricate relations between wetlands and human development pose serious challenges to any simple wetland policy. Highly generalized rules are often insensitive to the physical characteristics and dynamics of wetlands.

To some extent, the battle over wetlands has been a conflict between conservation and development. There is hardly a farmer, developer or shopping-mall builder in the U.S. who is not familiar with wetlands. The debate has pivoted around the problem of devising management strategies that provide certainty for developers while protecting the ecological features of wetlands. Fluctuating water levels and the sensitivity of wetlands to these changes as well as the dependence of wetlands on the surrounding landscape must consistently be taken into account.

Landowners understandably want to know the exact effect of wetland regulations when they construct a house or road. They want to know what activities will be allowed in which areas under what conditions. They want to be able to compensate for wetland losses at one site by restoring wetlands at other locations. And they want hard and fast rules, without surprises.

This need has led to proposals to take wetland policy out of the hands of the scientists and to establish simplistic rules through legislative fiat. Such attempts include congressional bill HR 1330, co-sponsored by 170 members of the House in 1992 and 100 members in 1993, which provides an example of science and legislation in conflict. The bill would require that hydric vegetation be present in every wetland. It also stipulates that wetlands be classified according to a once-and-for-all determination of a wetland's value or function.

In essence, HR 1330 treats wetlands like static water systems. (A similar problem of failing to recognize wetlands as a dynamic system was seen in the fall of 1991, when the U.S. administration tried and failed to redefine wetlands.) Moreover, the proposal would allow a landowner to select the time of year during which to decide whether or not a particular area constitutes a wetland. Because such hydric plants are missing at one time or another from most wetland sites, provisions of this kind could be used to define most wetlands out of existence.

The bill would require that federal agencies document 21 days of inundation or saturation for all wetlands. This artificial standard would be impossible to meet because water-level records are rarely available, and fluctuations are extremely difficult to predict. The expense of using modeling to foresee water levels is prohibitive: one study to determine the probability of a 100-year, or extremely rare, flood on about half the nation's floodplains cost more than $870 million.

Finally, the bill, which would allow for compensating the loss of one wetland by preserving another—called mitigation banking—ignores the tight associations between certain wetland functions and their watershed. A wetland's ability to control floodwater or maintain water quality can be seen immediately downstream. But, under the bill, downstream landowners are not compensated for the fact that their wetlands can no longer fulfill these functions. Further, because of their surroundings, two wetlands of similar size in different locations may have distinctly different attributes, functions and therefore value.

Scientifically sound management of wetlands that satisfies everyone is not easy to achieve, but there are signs of hope. In the past decade, investigators have learned much about defining and managing wetlands as dynamic features in the landscape. This knowledge could form the basis of a workable policy.

Recognizing the role of fluctuating water levels and the interrelation of the landscape is a first step.

Water levels vary within relatively well defined ranges in most wetlands and can therefore provide a foundation for definition and regulation. Soil and geologic information can be gathered to identify long-term shifts. Other criteria can help indicate altered or managed wetlands as well as those that are infrequently flooded. It is also important to consider the immediate landscape when the wetland is being evaluated.

In the future, natural processes should be preserved as much as possible. In general, people have attempted to control the rise and fall of rivers by building dams. When such fluctuations cannot be maintained, remedial management should be undertaken to simulate natural hydrologic pulses.

Regional watershed analyses that address not only present but future situations can help delineate wetlands. These analyses can form the foundation for planning and regulation. At the same time, protection of these systems can be integrated into broader land-use policies—including the management of water supplies and of floodplains, storm water and pollution.

Such scientifically sound policies have been implemented in many countries. In 1971 the Ramsar Convention called for the protection of wetlands and for the formulation of national plans to use them wisely. Today 37 million hectares at 582 sites have been designated as Ramsar sites—including 1.1 million hectares in the U.S. Nevertheless, only 74 nations have joined the convention.

Because of their special characteristics, wetlands pose difficult but not insurmountable challenges in terms of protection and restoration. If we recognize these features and incorporate them into policies at all levels of government, we can save the remaining wetlands, from the tropics to the tundra.

The Authors

Jon A. Kusler, William J. Mitsch and Joseph S. Larson work on aspects of wetland management and ecology. Kusler, who has advised many state and federal agencies on water resource policy, is executive director of the Association of Wetland Managers. Professor of natural resources and environmental science at Ohio State University, Mitsch has conducted extensive research on wetlands restoration and ecosystem modeling. Larson is professor at and director of the Environmental Institute at the University of Massachusetts at Amherst. He has studied, among other topics, the behavior of beavers and the assessment of freshwater wetlands.

The Endangered Species Act of 1973 was passed in response to concern about the global decline of species, and it is considered one of the most comprehensive wildlife conservation laws in the world. Its purpose is to "conserve the ecosystems upon which threatened or endangered species depend" and to conserve and recover species listed as either endangered or threatened. An endangered species is in danger of becoming extinct throughout all or a significant portion of its range (the geographic distribution of that species). A threatened species is likely to become endangered within the foreseeable future.

A key feature of the act is its explicit indifference to the cost required to remedy a listed species' status. However, the act also includes a rarely used clause that provides a remedy when protecting a species will have too great a cost in human terms. This clause allows a project developer, for example, to ask a special Endangered Species Committee to exempt the project from the provisions of the Endangered Species Act, although other protective measures are usually required instead. This committee is informally known as the God Squad because it has power over the life and death of listed species. However, in the act's long history, this clause has only been invoked three times, and the developer prevailed in only one of these.

Congress has amended the act three times, in 1978, 1982, and 1988, but the next article describes a new interpretation of its provisions that considers "ecosystem management," which focuses on preserving entire habitats rather than on a single species in isolation. —*RA*

"Endangered: One Endangered Species Act"
by Tim Beardsley
Scientific American, March 1995

Last December, Federal District Judge William L. Dwyer gave a legal thumbs-up to the Clinton administration's compromise plan for logging and conservation in federally owned forests of the Northwest. The program allows logging operations—which the judge halted in 1991— to recommence at reduced rates. It also establishes a mosaic of six different forms of logging-controlled areas. The strategy aims to guard not only species listed as threatened under the Endangered Species Act, such as the northern spotted owl and the marbled murrelet, but hundreds of other life-forms.

The verdict marked a crucial turning point in the protracted, bitter struggle between environmentalists and timber interests. Yet, in all probability, it will not be the last word. Biologists, who generally accept the agreement as a step in the right direction, disagree over how much it protects imperiled species. In addition, the plan relies on federal agencies to monitor habitats— something critics say government has failed to do.

Moreover, Congress may rewrite the very laws underlying the plan. Representative Don Young of Alaska, chairman of the Resources Committee in the House (known until this year as the Natural Resources Committee), has declared his immediate intention to rework the Endangered Species Act. Young, who has considerable influence, openly disdains efforts to protect rare plants and animals. He denies there is good evidence that the spotted owl is threatened, a view shared by the timber industry. David S. Wilcove of the Environmental Defense Fund, who argues that the owl in question has been better studied than almost any U.S. bird, says Young's position represents "a degree of denial worthy of inclusion in a psychology textbook."

Young further maintains that the act should compensate property owners who refrain from development because of its provisions. To many environmentalists, the cost of such a change would make the act untenable.

Congressional and legal assaults on the act could affect the outcome of any future challenges to the way in which the forestry plan is implemented. And, according to scientists, there are many ways its enactment could be less than perfect. E. Charles Meslow of the Wildlife Management Institute in Washington, D.C., contends the "agencies have never been able to accomplish the monitoring that's been specified."

Meslow says he can now see flaws in the plan that he helped to design. The scientific groups involved drew up 10 different options, each allowing various amounts of logging. Today Meslow believes that from the outset the administration had an unstated goal for the amount of timber to be harvested. "If we'd known that, we would have spent our time more wisely," Meslow explains.

The compromise breaks new ground by employing "ecosystem management." Rather than catering to every species that might cause concern, the approach focuses on preserving entire habitats. The pragmatic philosophy acknowledges the paucity of hard data on most affected creatures. "My opinion has always been that if we persisted in a species-by-species approach, society was not going to have enough patience," says Jerry F. Franklin, a professor at the University of Washington and a key player in the drafting of the plan.

Franklin points out that the view of many biologists that the spotted owl is in accelerated decline "is not completely accepted." He thinks environmentalists should be content to have achieved most of their objectives. "Taking extreme positions on the amount of protection needed is a pretty dangerous thing to do," he states. "A number of environmental scientists have not got the message yet."

The critics remain unconvinced. The plan estimates, for example, that the spotted owl and the marbled murrelet have more than a 80 percent chance of keeping a "well-distributed" population over the next 100 years. But Daniel Doak, a mathematical modeler at the University of California at Santa Cruz, disagrees. "There is a real question about whether there will be any owls left in the wild in 100 years' time to enjoy the nice landscape we're making for them," Doak declares.

Christopher A. Frissell, an aquatic ecologist at the University of Montana, complains that the Forest

Service deliberately decided not to scrutinize fish data. According to Frissell, findings indicate that several species may have less than a 50 percent chance of surviving under the agreement.

"There should be better consideration of species and stocks," concurs James R. Karr, director of the Institute for Environmental Studies at the University of Washington. The focus on habitats, he believes, means that threats to some species, particularly salmonid fish, have been overlooked because they occur outside the geographic scope of the compromise. The plan recognizes that hundreds of less well known terrestrial and aquatic species in the region may not survive the changes.

Despite the doubts, conservationists seemed ready in January to accept Dwyer's ruling. "It's a reasonable plan, and I want to be supportive," says Wilcove of the Environmental Defense Fund. But, among all the swirling uncertainties, one thing is sure: the legal and scientific scrutiny of wildlife and the government's actions in the Pacific Northwest is far from over.

To some, the Arctic National Wildlife Refuge (ANWR) has come to represent a last stand against the meaningless despoilment of an Arctic wilderness, while to others it could make the United States a little less dependent on foreign oil.

As W. Wayt Gibbs says in the following article, "The last great onshore oil field in America may lie beneath the nation's last great coastal wilderness preserve." The problem is, nobody knows to any useful degree how much oil the refuge holds, and that is the rub. The Alaska National Interest Lands Conservation Act of 1980 set aside 1.5 million acres inside the 19-million-acre reserve for possible oil and gas exploration and extraction. But almost from the beginning that purpose has been challenged. More recently, Congress tried to include an ANWR exploration provision in a national energy bill, which three times failed, in part because of the provision. The bill finally passed in 2005, stripped of the provision, but ANWR drilling measures continue to be raised in other proposed legislation.

Gibbs says science should enter the fray and use current, relatively noninvasive exploration techniques to estimate the size of the resource. "How the question is settled," he says, "will reveal something about the American public's priorities, its patience, and its tolerance for risk." —RA

"The Arctic Oil and Wildlife Refuge"
by W. Wayt Gibbs
Scientific American, May 2001

Flying from Deadhorse, Alaska, west to Phillips Petroleum's new Alpine oil field, you can watch the evolution of oil development on the North Slope scroll below like a time-lapse film. At takeoff, the scene fills with the mammoth field where it all began: Prudhoe Bay, discovered in 1968 and uncorked in 1977 to send its oil down the Trans-Alaska Pipeline to the ice-free port at Valdez.

Climbing higher, the plane tracks feeder pipelines that zig westward to Kuparuk, second only to Prudhoe among the most oil-rich onshore fields yet found in North America. Like Prudhoe, Kuparuk has grown since its opening in 1981 into a scattershot of gravel well pads connected over 800 square miles by a web of roads and pipes to giant processing plants, camp buildings, vehicle lots, and dark pits full of rock and mud drilled from the deep.

To the north, the artificial islands of Northstar and Endicott appear just offshore. And as the flight descends onto the airstrip at Alpine, you fast-forward to the state of the art in petroleum engineering. Industry executives often cite this nearly roadless, 94-acre project as a model of environmentally and financially responsible oil development, proof that oil companies have learned how to coexist with delicate Arctic ecosystems.

Alpine is the newest and westernmost of the North Slope oil fields, but not for long. When its valves opened in November 2000, crude oil flowed the 50 miles back to Pump Station 1 near Deadhorse—as all oil produced on the slope must—via a new tributary to the pipeline system. By February, Alpine's production

The Debate/*Oil vs. Wildlife*

- Senate bill S. 389 would open the coastal plain and foothills of the Arctic National Wildlife Refuge, the so-called 1002 Area, to oil development. A competing bill, S. 411, would designate the area as wilderness, prohibiting development.
- Geologists have used 1985 seismic data to esti-mate how much profitable oil and gas lie below the surface. But before any lease sale, oil companies would conduct new seismic surveys. That would leave a grid of visible scars in the vegetation of the plain but would have little or no effect on wildlife.
- Ice roads and exploration wells would follow. Fish and waterfowl may suffer if rivers and lakes are overdrained.
- A network of oil fields, processing plants and pipelines would extract the oil. A nearly roadless development may have little effect on the herd of 130,000 caribou that calves on the plain. Or it may displace the animals, affecting their nutrition, predation and birth rates, and long-term popu-lation growth.

had already hit the plant's maximum output of almost 90,000 barrels a day. But the pipe to Deadhorse can carry much more.

It was built with the future in mind, and from Alpine the future of the hydrocarbon industry on the North Slope heads in three directions at once. It will continue westward, into the 23-million-acre National Petroleum Reserve–Alaska (NPR-A) on which Alpine borders. The federal government put four million acres up for lease in 1999, and exploration began last year. New fields there will deliver their oil through Alpine's pipe.

The future may lead southward as well. Soaring gas prices spurred North Slope companies last year to commit $75 million to plan a $10-billion natural gas pipeline that would open some 35 trillion cubic feet of untapped reserves to the lower American states by the end of the decade.

Beyond 2010, Phillips, BP and the other Alaskan oil producers look toward the east for new opportunities. Not 30 miles past Badami, the eastern terminus of the North Slope infrastructure, lie the coastal plain and tussock tundra of the so-called 1002 Area. It is named for the section of the Alaska National Interest Lands Conservation Act of 1980 that set aside 1.5 million acres of federal property in deference to geologists' guesses that the region entombs billions of barrels of oil and trillions of cubic feet of gas.

The same act placed the 1002 Area inside the 19-million-acre Arctic National Wildlife Refuge (ANWR), in deference to biologists' observations that the coastal plain provides a premium Arctic habitat: calving ground for the Porcupine caribou herd; nesting and staging wetlands for tundra swans and other migratory waterfowl; dens for polar bears and arctic foxes; and year-round forage for a small herd of muskoxen.

Congress thus instigated one of the longest-running environmental turf wars of the past century, and the darts have again begun to fly. On February 26, Senator Frank H. Murkowski of Alaska introduced S. 389, a bill that would open the 1002 Area to oil and gas exploration and production. The bill allows the Bureau of Land Management to restrict the activities to ensure that they "will result in no significant adverse effect on the fish and wildlife, their habitat, subsistence resources and the environment."

Can careful regulation prevent such effects? Or does even the most compact, high-tech, thoroughly monitored oil development pose an unacceptable risk to the largest American wildlife refuge remaining so close to its natural condition?

It is a mistake to ask scientists questions that force them to weigh the relative values of oil and wilderness. Some 245 biologists, not waiting to be asked, signed an open letter to President Bill Clinton last November urging him to bypass Congress and declare the area a wilderness, which would close it to development. In interviews with numerous Alaskan petroleum geologists, on the other hand, virtually all asserted that the oil industry could move in without causing more than cosmetic damage. In a fundamentally political dispute, scientists' opinions should carry no more weight than anyone else's.

Science and engineering should enter the debate over the fate of the Arctic refuge, however—not as a lobby but as a source of facts that all positions must accommodate. Thirty years of innovation has produced less disruptive ways of finding and removing the oil below the tundra. And 25 years of biology has quantified how those activities disturb the life on its surface. Before the public decides the question, it should have the clearest picture possible of what it might gain, what it might risk in the gamble—and what uncertainties are tucked into the word "might."

What Lies Beneath

At least eight separate groups of geologists have tried over the years to guess how much oil and gas sit below the 1002 Area in forms and places that would allow them to be recovered with current technology and at realistic prices. All eight teams relied on a single set of data from a seismic survey made in the winters of 1984 and 1985. Long rows of low-frequency microphones were set down on the snow to capture the echoes of sound-generating trucks up to a mile away as the sound waves bounced off rock layers at various depths. The string of microphones was moved, the process was repeated, and 1,450 miles of cross-sectional snapshots were taken, covering the entire 1002 Area in a rough three-by-six-mile grid.

A Model of a Modern Major Oil Field

Removing oil from the Arctic refuge would probably require four or more Alpine-size fields. Processing plants, split into 1,500-ton modules, would be hauled on ice roads built with water removed from nearby lakes and sprayed on the frozen tundra. Each seven-foot-thick gravel pad, accessible summer only by air, would hold up to 60 closely spaced wellheads. Drilled by 150-foot-tall derricks or smaller coiled tubing rigs, the wells would penetrate the permafrost and then veer to run horizontally through

oil pockets up to six miles away. Half or more of the wells would inject seawater or natural gas into the rock to push oil toward producing wells nearby. A central processing facility would remove water and gas from the flow of satellite fields up to 30 miles distant, then pump all the oil through a pipeline to Prudhoe Bay. The pipe could be buried under rivers and elevated five feet above the tundra to allow caribou and muskoxen to pass. Regularly spaced "loops" would halt flow automatically if a large leak occurred. About 300 crew members would run the facility year-round.

In wintertime, large convoys of roughly 100 workers, eight to 10 sound-generating trucks and three dozen other vehicles would crisscross the frozen tundra, shooting seismic surveys. Other teams of 100 or so would pour ice pads, drive two-million-pound mobile drill rigs onto them, then rush to complete wildcat wells before the spring thaw in April.

Turning those recordings into pictures of the subsurface and then inferring from the pictures which formations hold what quantity of oil is as much an art as it is a science. "The source rocks, trap formations [that hold the oil in place] and extent of migration all must be estimated based on analogies and prior experience," explains Mark D. Myers, director of the oil and gas division of Alaska's Department of Natural Resources.

Wesley K. Wallace, a geologist at the University of Alaska, Fairbanks (U.A.F.), ticks off more unknowns: "size of the formation, thickness, porosity—each has an error bar," sometimes a very large one, and even the size of the error bars is subjective.

No wonder, then, that the eight independent studies arrived at widely divergent estimates. Differences in their methods make it useless to compare them. But by all accounts, the best assessment to date is the latest one, led by Kenneth J. Bird of the U.S. Geological Survey (USGS). From 1996 to 1998 Bird and his teammates ran the old seismic data through new computer models. They gathered logs and rock samples from 41 wells drilled over the years near the borders of the refuge. They looked again at outcrops where oil-stained rock breaks through the permafrost and traveled to the adjacent mountains where some likely reservoir strata are uplifted and exposed. And they looked at the reflectance of vitrinite and the tracks made by radioactive nuclei in apatite found in the 1002 Area for clues to those minerals' temperature history, which matters because hydrocarbons turn into oil only when cooked just so.

The result is not one estimate but several, because the relevant figure is not how much oil is there but how much can be profitably recovered—and that depends in turn on the price of oil. Bird's group concluded that thorough exploration would most likely yield about seven billion barrels (bbo) of economically recoverable oil if North Slope prices remain above $24 a barrel, where they were in March. The estimate falls to about 5 bbo if oil prices slip to $18, and it plummets to a few hundred million barrels if prices drop to $12. Since 1991 the price of North Slope crude has fluctuated between $9 and $35, averaging $18 a barrel.

At 7 bbo, the 1002 Area would hold about half as much profitable petroleum as Prudhoe Bay did in 1977. But as with Prudhoe, the oil could be raised only over the course of several decades, following a classic bell-shaped curve. Industry insiders say that 10 years would probably pass between a decision to open the refuge to development and the first flow into the Alaskan pipeline. Environmental-impact studies and hearings would take two years, if the history of NPR-A is a guide. Companies would then have a year or two to do more intense seismic surveys and to prepare their bids on leases. Several years of exploration typically go into each discovery—after two years of drilling in NPR-A, for example, no strikes have been announced yet. Each permanent drilling site, processing facility and pipeline extension would have to clear more environmental analyses and hearings, and each would take two to three years to build.

An analysis by the U.S. Energy Information Administration (EIA) suggests that if the USGS estimate of 7 bbo is correct, then the 1002 Area will generate fewer than 200,000 barrels a day for the first five years. The EIA also forecasts that American petroleum consumption, 19.5 million barrels a day last year, will rise to 23 million by 2010, with 66 percent of that amount imported. At its peak, probably no earlier than 2030, complete development of the coastal plain of the Arctic refuge would produce about one million barrels of oil a day. Flow from the 1002 Area would then meet something shy of 4 percent of the nation's daily demand for petroleum [*see box on page 113*].

There's the Rub

Petroleum geologists know what they need to do to reduce the huge uncertainties in the USGS analysis. "The first thing a company would do is shoot a new 3-D seismic survey," Myers says. With gaps in the previous seismic data of up to six miles wide, "every prospect drilled on the slope this year would be invisible on that [1985] survey," he observes. This time "the grid would be much finer," with lines spaced about 1,100 feet apart, says Michael Faust, geoscience technology manager for Phillips in Anchorage. With new, high-resolution data, supercomputers could model the subsurface in three-dimensional detail.

The caravan of survey equipment, however, would appear much the same as before, Faust says: typically, eight vibrating and seven recording vehicles, accompanied by personnel carriers, mechanic trucks, mobile shop trucks, fuel tankers, an incinerator, plus a crew of 80 to 120 people and a camp train of 20 to 25 shipping containers on skis, pulled by several Caterpillar tractors on treads. The crew would leave in January and stay out through April, returning the next winter if necessary to cover the entire 1002 Area,

1,100 feet at a time. Each interested oil company or partnership would shoot its own complete survey, employing its own caravan.

That prospect worries Martha K. Raynolds, a U.A.F. biologist. She and Janet C. Jorgenson, a botanist with the U.S. Fish and Wildlife Service in Fairbanks, have returned six times to monitor 200 patches of tundra that were randomly chosen for study as the last seismic vehicles passed over them 17 years ago. Ten percent still showed scuffing or reduced plant cover after 10 years, and 7 percent—about 100 miles of trail—had not recovered by 1998.

The problem, they say, is the terrain. The wide, low-pressure tires of the seismic trucks leave little trace on the flat, frozen, snow-covered grasslands around Prudhoe Bay and Alpine. Rubber treads on the tractors grip well enough. But east toward ANWR, the mountains march northward and the coast withdraws. That leaves the North Slope just 20 to 30 miles within the 1002 Area to attempt its typically gentle decline from rolling foothills to stream-crazed plateau to the ice-locked Beaufort Sea. Often it fails, and the tundra piles into hummocks. Winds clear the snow from their tops, exposing the dwarf willows and the standing dead vegetation. Tires and skis crush the shrubs and compact the sedges. Rubber treads lose traction on slopes, are replaced with steel and inevitably dig in, Jorgenson says.

At breakup in May, permafrost below the compacted areas thaws early, deprived of its usual insulation. Pools form, some native plant species die, and visitors take over. Three quarters of the vegetative scars were still visible from the air a decade after the survey; many appear to be permanent. But no research suggests that the changes affect wildlife, both scientists say.

What Harm in Looking?

Seismic surveys generate clues, not discoveries. For petroleum geologists, truth emerges only from holes in the ground. Once the supercomputers have spit out their images, exploration teams would fan out across the frozen 1002 Area to drill wildcat wells. A mobile drill rig like the one at Alpine weighs 2.2 million pounds, so it is driven and parked on thick slabs of ice made by laying down six-inch-deep piles of ice chips and cementing them with water.

With lots of water, in fact—about a million gallons per mile of road. Around Prudhoe, tens of thousands of lakes ensure that liquid water is plentiful even when the air drops to –20 degrees Fahrenheit. Twelve years ago, however, a thorough search of the 1002 Area in April—when the ice hits its maximum thickness of seven feet—turned up only nine million gallons of liquid water sequestered in ice pockets along 237 miles of the major interior rivers. Steve Lyons, chief hydrologist for the refuge, found 255 lakes, ponds and puddles within the 1002 Area. Just 59 of those were deeper than seven feet, and only eight contained enough unfrozen water to build a mile or more of ice road. The largest basins lie in the Canning and Jago river

Facts/*Forecasting the Flow*

- Full development of the 1002 Area would most likely produce about seven billion barrels of profitable oil, according to a 1998 analysis by the U.S. Geological Survey, but only if North Slope oil prices remain above $24 a barrel.
- If the refuge were opened to exploration this year, oil production from the area would probably begin around 2010.
- The flow of oil would rise to a peak rate around 2030 of roughly one million barrels a day—just under 4 percent of U.S. daily consumption—according to the USGS analysis. An independent estimate by Jean Laherrère of Petroconsultants in Geneva put the peak flow at just over 700,000 barrels a day, however.
- ANWR also probably holds about four trillion cubic feet of natural gas within the 1002 Area, the USGS estimates. Gas production would require construction of a new gas pipeline to connect the North Slope to the lower 48 states.

deltas, and their bottom water is often brackish and potentially poisonous to vegetation.

Allow those few wet lakes to freeze through in winter, Lyons predicts, and next summer the waterfowl that pause in their migration to feed on invertebrates in the ponds will find fewer to eat. Draw too heavily from the spring-fed Canning, which runs free year-round, and the many kinds of fish that overwinter there may suffer, he warns.

"Water in ANWR could be a problem," says Thomas Manson, the environmental manager at Alpine, which treats and recycles its freshwater but still runs through 70,000 gallons every day. The trouble is not only quantity but also distribution: as a rule, water is drawn no farther than 10 miles from where it is needed, or else it freezes in the trucks on the way. Lyons admits that there may be technological solutions, such as a desalinization plant connected to a heated, elevated pipeline. But such measures would change the economics of the enterprise and thus the amount of oil recoverable.

(Wild)Life Goes On

Of course, if any oil is to be recovered, plants must be built. "Put four or five Alpine-size fields into ANWR with the processing facilities to support them, and you're talking about a few thousand acres of development," Myers says. "Clearly, some habitat will be damaged or destroyed. The question is: How will that modify the behavior of the animals?"

Theoretically, oil development could affect animals in many ways. Drillers no longer dump their cuttings and sewage and garbage into surface pits; these are now either burned or injected deep into wells. That greatly reduces the impact on foxes and bears. But there are other emissions. Alpine sees six to eight aircraft pass through every day, some as large as a C-130 Hercules. The scents of up to 700 workers and the noise of numerous trucks and two enormous turbines, big as the engines of a 747, constantly waft out over the tundra. A 10-foot gas flare shimmers atop a 100-foot stack. And three pipelines—two bringing seawater and diesel fuel in, one pumping crude out—fly to the horizon at just over the height of a caribou's antlers.

How the animal inhabitants of the 1002 Area would react to a collection of Alpine-style oil developments is a puzzle to which biologists have only pieces of a solution. Some wildlife does seem to have been displaced around the oil fields at Prudhoe and Kuparuk. Tundra swans, for example, tend to nest more than 650 feet from the roadways there, and caribou with calves typically hang back 2.5 miles or more.

Brad Griffith of U.A.F.'s Institute of Arctic Biology recently found two important patterns in the distribution since 1985 of the 130,000 caribou of the Porcupine herd, which arrives in the 1002 Area almost every year by June to bear and wean its young before departing for warmer climes by mid-July. The first pattern is a strong correlation of calf survival with the amount of high-protein food in the calving area. Second, caribou cows with newborns have consistently concentrated in the most rapidly greening areas (as measured by satellite) during lactation. Scott Wolfe, a graduate student of Griffith's, last year showed that the second pattern holds as well for the half of the Central Arctic herd that calves east of the Sagavanirktok River.

Across that river lie the big oil fields, and Wolfe found that from 1987 to 1995 the western half of the herd shifted its calving concentrations southward, away from the growing development and the richest forage. Ray Cameron, another Institute biologist, worries that that movement may affect the caribou numbers strongly enough to be perceptible above the normal fluctuations caused by weather, insect cycles and many other factors. It hasn't yet: at 27,000, the Central Arctic herd is five times as large as it was in 1978.

But in a 1995 study Cameron and others reported data showing that a 20-pound drop in the weight of the mother could lower calf survival by 20 percent and fertility by 30 percent. Cameron also tracked down radio-tagged cows and found that those that summered among the oil fields bore 23 percent fewer calves on average than their counterparts east of the river. But a critical link in this logical chain is missing: evidence that caribou, pushed off their preferred forage, don't get enough to eat.

Caribou in ANWR might suffer more than the Central Arctic herd has, because almost five times as many animals there forage in an area one fifth the size of the plain surrounding Prudhoe and Kuparuk. With fewer options, a larger fraction of the caribou cows may lose weight and bear fewer young. Oil fields could push more of them into the foothills, where calves are most likely to fall prey to eagles, wolves or bears. Griffith and his colleagues recently combined satellite imagery with caribou-calving and grizzly-bear-tracking data from the 1002 Area into a computer model. It predicts that pushing the caribou calving concentration toward the foothills would reduce annual calf survival by 14 percent on average, Griffith says.

And Fish and Wildlife Service biologist Patricia Reynolds, who monitors the 250 muskoxen that live within the 1002 Area, points out that those animals survive the brutal winters on the plain primarily by moving little and conserving stored fat. If oil workers mine gravel from the riverbanks where they stand, the muskoxen will bolt, upsetting a precariously balanced energy budget and jeopardizing their young.

On the other hand, if the drill pads are served by short airstrips rather than long networks of roads, the caribou may fear them less and suffer little displacement. Wells no longer need be directly above the reservoir, so drill pads could be placed to avoid the most nutritious cottongrass patches. Many of the muskoxen wear radio collars, so pains could be taken to avoid them.

All things considered, the wildlife would probably cope. The question is, could we? Science itself may have a vested interest in thwarting S. 389, suggests John W. Schoen, senior scientist with the Audubon Society in Anchorage. "If global climate is changing, its effects will be most magnified in northern latitudes, in places like the Arctic refuge," he argues. "How are we going to measure these subtle changes and sort out which are due to industrial development versus which are due to global climate change? One way is to protect some areas as experimental controls. The Arctic refuge would certainly serve as such a laboratory—if it remains intact."

In fact, the 1002 Area is already the centerpiece of a long and revealing experiment—a social and political experiment that may at last be approaching its conclusion. How the question is settled will reveal something about the American public's priorities, its patience, and its tolerance for risk.

3 Tragic Combatants: Trade and the Environment

The following article by Marguerite Holloway describes a rift between global business and U.S. environmentalists. It recounts the conflict between a U.S. law aimed at protecting endangered sea turtles and a World Trade Organization (WTO) ruling that says the law, as interpreted, is a barrier to trade. The 1989 law bans shrimp purchases unless the nets that caught them use "turtle-excluder devices." Originally applied to Caribbean and western Atlantic shrimpers, the law was extended worldwide after several environmental groups sued the U.S. government. Following several iterations of court rulings and government attempts to comply, the U.S. government finally decided that it could buy shrimps from four Asian trading partners (Thailand, India, Malaysia, and Pakistan) only if they adopted similar turtle protection regulations and enforced them.

The United States also lost its appeal of the WTO ruling in late 1998, after Holloway's article was published. The appeal report clarified that

the U.S. law was recognized as valid by the WTO
but that it had been applied unfairly. The United
States had provided some countries—notably
those in the Caribbean—with technical and
financial aid and longer transition periods for
their fishers to start using turtle-excluder devices
but didn't give the same advantages to the four
Asian countries that had filed the complaint with
the WTO. —RA

"Trade Rules"
by Marguerite Holloway
Scientific American, August 1998

The 1990s have seen the emergence of a conciliatory credo: business and environmental interests are not just compatible, they are inextricable. A healthy environment and natural-resource base are prerequisites for a healthy economy; a smoothly functioning world market, in turn, produces the resources and mind-set needed to protect the environment. Concepts such as "sustainable development" and "eco-labeling" have accordingly promised consumers a hand in making the market environmentally accountable.

Although the rhetoric seems reasonable to many on both sides of the divide, it is proving difficult to implement. As an April decision by the World Trade Organization (WTO) indicates, the interests of one nation's consumers may be consistently forced to yield to the interests of free trade. The ruling stated that a U.S. law prohibiting the import of shrimp caught in nets that can entrap sea turtles was a barrier to trade. According to the WTO, the U.S. must import shrimp from Thailand, Malaysia, India and Pakistan—regardless of whether the harvests endanger sea turtles—or face large fines.

The WTO ruling—which the U.S. says it will appeal—is not the first to subsume a nation's environmental laws or its consumers' desires to the demands of global markets. Europeans are legally required to import U.S. hormone-treated beef, Americans must stomach tuna from Mexico that endangers dolphins, and the U.S. Environmental Protection Agency lowered air-quality standards to allow imports of reformulated gasoline. The shrimp ruling, however, has mobilized the environmental community in an unprecedented fashion.

Part of the reason is that all seven species of sea turtle are endangered. Populations of these mysterious, long-lived creatures have plummeted in the past 50 years. But the other stimulus for the outcry is a growing concern over the WTO's environmental mores and the role of so-called processing and production methods. Greatly simplified, trade law states that one country cannot exclude another's product if it is "like" most such products. Therefore, the U.S. cannot ban Asian shrimp if it looks and tastes like other shrimp. The production method is not a consideration. "That is a distinction that the trade system does not want to recognize," explains Daniel A. Seligman of the Sierra Club. And it is on precisely that distinction that eco-labeling and consumer choice hinge: Was wood harvested sustainably? Did shrimpers harm an endangered species?

"Industry has increasingly been arguing that labeling is a trade barrier because it establishes different standards," Seligman continues. In other words, if rulings such as this one continue to hold, trade could lose some of its power to enact environmental change. At the same time, the WTO ruling hardly represents a black-and-white case of trade trumping environment. Just as Americans resist being force-fed a product, the Asian countries are resisting U.S. efforts to force its domestic law down their throats. Further complicating the issue is the murky history of the U.S. position: the Clinton administration finds itself defending a legal interpretation it did not countenance in the first place.

The shrimp conflict has its roots in Public Law 101-162, Section 609, which the federal government enacted in 1989. The statute stated that the U.S. would not buy shrimp caught in nets without turtle-excluder devices, or TEDs. These grills sit in the necks of shrimpers' nets, allowing small crustaceans through but stopping larger creatures and diverting them out of the trap. By 1993 the government had effectively applied the law to fishermen plying the Caribbean and western Atlantic. (U.S. shrimpers had been required to use TEDs since 1987.)

As applied, the law did little to protect sea turtles worldwide. Shrimp caught in Asia, for example, was not prohibited from U.S. markets. So several organizations, including the Earth Island Institute, challenged the government, claiming that catches of all wild shrimp come under the law's jurisdiction. In December 1995 the U.S. Court of International Trade agreed: the U.S. must embargo all shrimp caught in TED-less nets.

The government then interpreted the law to mean that foreign imports should be checked on a shipment-by-shipment basis. But the plaintiffs argued that such checking does not protect sea turtles, because TED-less boats could hand off their catch to TED-certified trawlers.

So, in October 1996, the trade court ruled against the shipment-by-shipment interpretation. (The future of the ruling is unclear, as it was recently vacated, or annulled, during appeal.) Thus, American law mandated that other countries set up and enforce regulations requiring TEDs if they wanted access to the U.S. market. Countries were given a few months to do so.

Things quickly became dicey. Thailand—which already used TEDs—joined India, Malaysia and Pakistan in opposing the ban. These nations argued that the U.S. had no right to mandate their domestic policy and that the U.S. had not approached them to negotiate an agreement. "To me, this is perfectly reasonable for these four countries to say this is something that we do not buy and we will not do it," says Jagdish N. Bhagwati, a professor of economics at Columbia University. "The great advantage of rulings like this is that it forces the U.S. to go talk to countries and get into some discussion with the countries."

Such discussion did take place with Caribbean and Latin American nations. An Inter-American Convention on the Protection and Conservation of Sea Turtles was drafted in 1996; as of this spring, only six of the original 25 had signed it, however. "Multilateral agreement is the way to go," agrees Deborah T. Crouse, formerly of the Center for Marine Conservation. "But it is also much slower and more labor intensive. It took two years to get the Inter-American Convention, and the U.S. has not ratified or implemented it."

None of the four Asian countries contest that sea turtles are endangered. Several have conservation efforts in place, such as closing beaches to allow nesting, and have sought out TED training courses. Each has also signed the Convention on International Trade in Endangered Species (CITES), which lists all sea turtles as threatened.

But it is the muddy legal area where the WTO and CITES—as well as other environmental treaties—intersect that concerns environmentalists. CITES prohibits the trade of endangered species; the WTO prohibits barriers to trade such as objections to processing and production methods. What should happen when a production method threatens an endangered species? The WTO offers nothing but ambiguity on this front.

Formed in 1995 to replace the General Agreement on Tariffs and Trade (GATT), the WTO does make environmental provisions. The preamble to its charter mentions sustainable development; Article XX of GATT, which still holds for the WTO, offers exceptions to the rule of free trade; and the organization set up the Committee on Trade and the Environment. But that committee has not clarified the relation between the WTO and international environmental treaties.

Some lawyers point out that CITES, the Basel Convention (which prohibits the export of hazardous waste) and the Montreal Protocol (which limits chloro-fluorocarbon sales) could be interpreted as illegal under the WTO: each presents barriers to trade. And the legality of consumer choice—particularly as expressed through eco-labeling—remains just as unresolved. Even given its idiosyncratic intricacies, the WTO shrimp ruling suggests that trade and the environment are still far from being happily united.

The next two articles present arguments for and against free trade, cast largely as a matter involving environmental values. In the first article, Jagdish Bhagwati expresses regret that "the proponents of two of the great causes of the 1990s, trade and the environment, should be locked in combat," a conflict he says is "largely gratuitous."

Bhagwati says one reason environmentalists oppose free trade is to use trade policy "to impose their values on other communities and countries," a sort of "eco-imperialism." He uses the example of tuna trade between the United States and Mexico to illustrate. In 1992, a panel from the General Agreement on Tariffs and Trade (GATT) ruled that the United States couldn't suspend Mexico's trading rights simply because Mexico's purse seines killed dolphins in numbers and manners that violated U.S. laws. The U.S. action exposes values that are "idiosyncratic" and "not widely accepted," he said, and they put the "interests of the dolphin ahead of those of Mexico's people, who could prosper through more productive fishing." Further, unilateral sanctions based on the production methods of the other country would undermine the openness of the trading system and could lead to a "Pandora's box of protectionism."

The Mexico tuna trade continues to be an active issue. In 1995, a compromise was reached to allow import of the tuna, and a possible weakening of the federal "dolphin safe" tuna labeling program that indicated which tuna products didn't involve the netting of dolphins with purse seines. In 2002, the federal government weakened "dolphin-safe" fishing provisions, but

*two years later, a federal judge struck down the
decision. —RA*

"The Case for Free Trade"
by Jagdish Bhagwati
Scientific American, November 1993

Economists are reconciled to the conflict of absolutes:
that is why they invented the concept of trade-offs. It
should not surprise them, therefore, that the objective
of environmental protection should at times run
afoul of the goal of seeking maximum gains from
trade. In fact, economists would be suspicious of any
claims, such as those made by soothsaying politicians,
that both causes would be only mutually beneficial.
They are rightly disconcerted, however, by the passion
and the ferocity, and hence often the lack of logic or
facts, with which environmental groups have recently
assailed both free trade and the General Agreement on
Tariffs and Trade (GATT), the institution that oversees
the world trading system.

The environmentalists' antipathy to trade is perhaps
inevitable. Trade has been central to economic thinking
since Adam Smith discovered the virtues of specialization and of the markets that naturally sustain it.
Because markets do not normally exist for the pursuit
of environmental protection, they must be specially
created. Trade therefore suggests abstention from
governmental intervention, whereas environmentalism
suggests its necessity. Then again, trade is exploited

and its virtues extolled by corporate and multinational interests, whereas environmental objectives are embraced typically by nonprofit organizations, which are generally wary of these interests. Trade is an ancient occupation, and its nurture is the objective of institutions crafted over many years of experience and reflection. Protection of the environment, on the other hand, is a recent preoccupation of national and international institutions that are nascent and still evolving.

Last year the environmentalists' hostility to trade exploded in outrage when an impartial GATT Dispute Settlement Panel ruled in favor of Mexico and free trade and against the U.S. and the welfare of the dolphin. The U.S. had placed an embargo on the import of Mexican tuna on the grounds that the fish had been caught in purse-seine nets, which kill dolphins cruelly and in greater numbers than U.S. law permits. The GATT panel ruled, in effect, that the U.S. could not suspend Mexico's trading rights by proscribing unilaterally the methods by which that country harvested tuna.

This decision spurred the conservationists' subsequent campaigns against free trade and GATT. GATT has no shortage of detractors, of course. In fact, some of its recent critics have feared its impotence and declared it "dead," referring to it as the General Agreement to Talk and Talk. But the environmentalist attacks, which presume instead GATT's omnipotence, are something else again.

An advertisement by a coalition of environmental groups in the *New York Times* on April 20, 1992, set a new standard for alarmist, even scurrilous, writing, calculated to appeal to one's instincts rather than one's intellect. It talks of "faceless GATT bureaucrats" mounting a "sneak attack on democracy." This veiled reference to Pearl Harbor provides an example of a common tactic in trade controversy: Japan-bashing. The innuendos have continued unabated and are manifest in the endless battles in Congress over the supplemental environmental accords for the North American Free Trade Agreement (NAFTA). The hostility is also intruding on the conclusion of the Uruguay Round of GATT talks, now in their seventh year, with the environmentalists opposing the establishment of the new Multilateral Trade Organization, which is meant to provide effective discipline and a necessary institutional structure for GATT.

It is surely tragic that the proponents of two of the great causes of the 1990s, trade and the environment, should be locked in combat. The conflict is largely gratuitous. There are at times philosophical differences between the two that cannot be reconciled, as when some environmentalists assert nature's autonomy, whereas most economists see nature as a handmaiden to humankind. For the most part, however, the differences derive from misconceptions. It is necessary to dissect and dismiss the more egregious of these fallacies before addressing the genuine problems.

The fear is widespread among environmentalists that free trade increases economic growth and that growth harms the environment. That fear is misplaced.

Growth enables governments to tax and to raise resources for a variety of objectives, including the abatement of pollution and the general protection of the environment. Without such revenues, little can be achieved, no matter how pure one's motives may be.

How do societies actually spend these additional revenues? It depends on how getting rich affects the desire for a better environment. Rich countries today have more groups worrying about environmental causes than do poor countries. Efficient policies, such as freer trade, should generally help environmentalism, not harm it.

If one wants to predict what growth will do to the environment, however, one must also consider how it will affect the production of pollution. Growth affects not only the demand for a good environment but also the supply of the pollution associated with growth. The net effect on the environment will therefore depend on the kind of economic growth. Gene M. Grossman and Alan B. Krueger of Princeton University found that in cities around the world sulfur dioxide pollution fell as per capita income rose. The only exception was in countries whose per capita incomes fell below $5,000. In short, environmentalists are in error when they fear that trade, through growth, will necessarily increase pollution.

Economic effects besides those attributable to rising incomes also help to protect the environment. For example, freer trade enables pollution-fighting technologies available elsewhere to be imported. Thus, trade in low-sulfur-content coal will enable the users of local high-sulfur-content coal to shift from the latter to the former.

Free trade can also lead to better environmental outcomes from a shift in the composition of production. An excellent example is provided by Robert C. Feenstra of the University of California at Davis. He has shown how the imposition of restraints on Japanese automobile exports to the U.S. during the 1980s shifted the composition of those exports from small to large cars, as the Japanese attempted to increase their revenues without increasing the number of units they sold. Yet the large cars were fuel inefficient. Thus, protective efforts by the U.S. effectively increased the average amount of pollution produced by imported cars, making it more likely that pollution from cars would increase rather than diminish in the U.S.

Although these erroneous objections to free trade are readily dismissed (but not so easily eliminated from public discourse), there are genuine conflicts between trade and the environment. To understand and solve them, economists draw a distinction between two kinds of environmental problems: those that are intrinsically domestic and those that are intrinsically transnational.

Should Brazil pollute a lake lying wholly within its borders, the problem would be intrinsically domestic. Should it pollute a river that flows into Argentina, the matter would take on an intrinsically transnational character. Perhaps the most important examples of transnational pollution are acid rain, created when sulfur dioxide emissions in one country precipitate into rain in another, and greenhouse gases, such as carbon dioxide, which contribute to global warming wherever they are emitted.

Why do intrinsically domestic environmental questions create international concern? The main reason is the belief that diversity in environmental standards may affect competitiveness. Businesses and labor unions worry that their rivals in other countries may gain an edge if their governments impose lower standards of environmental protection. They decry such differences as unfair. To level the playing field, these lobbies insist that foreign countries raise their standards up to domestic ones. In turn, environmental groups worry that if such "harmonization up" is not undertaken prior to freeing trade, pressures from uncompetitive businesses at home will force down domestic standards, reversing their hard-won victories. Finally, there is the fear, dramatized by H. Ross Perot in his criticisms of NAFTA that factories will relocate to the countries whose environmental standards are lowest.

But if the competitiveness issue makes the environmentalists, the businesses and the unions into allies, the environmentalists are on their own in other ways. Two problem areas can be distinguished. First, some environmentalists are keen to impose their own ethical preferences on others, using trade sanctions to induce or coerce acceptance of such preferences. For instance, tuna fishing with purse-seine nets that kill dolphins is opposed by U.S. environmental groups, which consequently favor restraints on the importation of such tuna from Mexico and elsewhere. Second, other environmentalists fear that the rules of free trade, as embodied in GATT and strengthened in the Uruguay Round, will constrain their freedom to pursue even purely domestic environmental objectives, with GATT tribunals outlawing disputed regulation.

Environmentalists have cause for concern. Not all concerns are legitimate, however, and not all the solutions to legitimate concerns are sensible. Worry over competitiveness has thus led to the illegitimate demand that environmental standards abroad be treated as "social dumping." Offending countries are regarded as unfairly subsidizing their exporters through lax environmental requirements. Such implicit subsidies, the reasoning continues, ought to be offset by import duties.

Yet international differences in environmental standards are perfectly natural. Even if two countries share the same environmental objectives, the *specific* pollutions they would attack, and hence the industries they would hinder, will generally not be identical. Mexico has a greater social incentive than does the U.S. to spend an extra dollar preventing dysentery rather than reducing lead in gasoline.

Equally, a certain environmental good might be valued more highly by a poor country than by a rich one.

Contrast, for instance, the value assigned to a lake with the cost of cleaning up effluents discharged into it by a pharmaceutical company. In India such a lake's water might be drunk by a malnourished population whose mortality would increase sharply with the rise in pollution. In the U.S. the water might be consumed by few people, all of whom have the means to protect themselves with privately purchased water filters. In this example, India would be the more likely to prefer clean water to the pharmaceutical company's profits.

The consequences of differing standards are clear: each country will have less of the industry whose pollution it fears relatively more than other countries do. Indeed, even if there were no international trade, we would be shrinking industries whose pollution we deter. This result follows from the policy of forcing polluters of all stripes to pay for the harm they cause. To object, then, to the effects our negative valuation of pollution have on a given industry is to be in contradiction: we would be refusing to face the consequences of our environmental preferences.

Nevertheless, there is sentiment for enacting legislation against social dumping. Senator David L. Boren of Oklahoma, the proponent of the International Pollution Deterrence Act of 1991, demanded import duties on the grounds that "some U.S. manufacturers, such as the U.S. carbon and steel alloy industry, spend as much as 250 percent more on environmental controls as a percentage of gross domestic product than do other countries. . . . I see the unfair advantage enjoyed by other nations exploiting the environment and public health for economic gain when I look at many industries important to my own state." Similarly, Vice President Al Gore wrote in *Earth in the Balance: Ecology and the Human Spirit* that "just as government subsidies of a particular industry are sometimes considered unfair under the trade laws, weak and ineffectual enforcement of pollution control measures should also be included in the definition of unfair trading practices."

These demands betray lack of economic logic, and they ignore political reality as well. Remember that the so-called subsidy to foreign producers through lower standards is not given but only implied. According to Senator Boren, the subsidy would be calculated as "the cost that would have to be incurred by the manufacturer or producer of the foreign articles of merchandise to comply with environmental standards imposed on U.S. producers of the same class of merchandise." Anyone familiar with the way dumping calculations are made knows that the Environmental Protection Agency could come up with virtually any estimates it cared to produce. Cynical politics would inevitably dictate the calculations.

Still, there may be political good sense in assuaging environmentalists' concerns about the relocation of factories to countries with lower standards. The governments of higher-standards countries could do so without encumbering free trade by insisting that their businesses accede to the higher standards when they go abroad. Such a policy lies entirely within the jurisdictional powers of a higher-standards country. Moreover, the governments of lower-standards countries would be most unlikely to object to such an act of good citizenship by the foreign investors.

Environmentalists oppose free trade for yet another reason: they wish to use trade policy to impose their values on other communities and countries. Many environmentalists want to suspend the trading rights of countries that sanction the use of purse-seine nets in tuna fishing and of leg-hold traps in trapping. Such punishments seem an inappropriate use of state power, however. The values in question are not widely accepted, such as human rights, but idiosyncratic. One wonders when the opponents of purse-seine nets put the interests of the dolphin ahead of those of Mexico's people, who could prosper through more productive fishing. To borrow the campaign manifesto of President Bill Clinton: Should we not put people first?

Moreover, once such values intrude on free trade, the way is opened for an endless succession of demands. Environmentalists favor dolphins; Indians have their sacred cows. Animal-rights activists, who do not prefer one species over another, will object to our slaughterhouses.

The moral militancy of environmentalists in the industrialized world has begun to disillusion their closest counterparts in the undeveloped countries. These local environmentalists accuse the rich countries of "eco-imperialism," and they deny that the Western nations have a monopoly on virtue. The most radical of today's proenvironment magazines in India, *Down to Earth*, editorialized recently: "In the current world reality trade is used as an instrument entirely by Northern countries to discipline environmentally errant nations. Surely, if India or Kenya were to threaten to stop trade with the U.S., it would hardly affect the latter. But the fact of the matter is that it is the Northern countries that have the greatest [adverse] impact on the world's environment."

If many countries were to play this game, then repeated suspensions of trading rights would begin to undermine the openness of the trading system and the predictability and stability of international markets. Some environmentalists assert that each country should be free to insist on the production methods of its trading partners. Yet these environmentalists ignore the certain consequence of their policy: a Pandora's box of protectionism would open up. Rarely are production methods in an industry identical in different countries.

There are certainly better ways to indulge the environmentalists' propensity to export their ethical preferences. The U.S. environmental organizations can lobby in Mexico to persuade its government to adopt their views. Private boycotts can also be undertaken. In fact, boycotts can carry much clout in rich countries with big markets, on which the targeted poor countries often depend. The frequent and enormously expensive advertisements by environmental groups against GATT show also that their resources far exceed those of the cash-strapped countries whose policies they oppose.

Cost-benefit analysis leads one to conclude that unilateral governmental suspension of others' trading rights is not an appropriate way to promote one's lesser ethical preferences. Such sanctions can, on the other hand, appropriately be invoked multilaterally to defend universal moral values. In such cases—as in the censure of apartheid, as practiced until recently in South Africa—it is possible to secure widespread agreement for sanctions. With a large majority converted to the cause, GATT's waiver procedure can be used to suspend the offending country's trading rights.

Environmentalists are also worried about the obstacles that the current and prospective GATT rules pose for environmental regulations aimed entirely at domestic production and consumption. In principle, GATT lets a country enforce any regulation that does not discriminate against or among foreign suppliers. One can, for example, require airbags in cars, provided that the rule applies to all automobile makers. GATT even permits rules that discriminate against trade for the purpose of safety and health.

GATT, however, recognizes three ways in which regulations may be set in gratuitous restraint of trade; in following procedures aimed at avoiding such outcomes, GATT upsets the environmentalists. First, the true intention—and effect—of a regulation may be to protect not the environment but local business. Second, a country may impose more restrictions than necessary to achieve its stated environmental objective. Third, it may set standards that have no scientific basis.

The issue of intentions is illustrated by the recently settled "beer war" between Ontario and the U.S. Five years ago the Canadian province imposed a 10-cents-a-can tax on beer, ostensibly to discourage littering. The U.S. argued that the law in fact intended to discriminate against its beer suppliers, who used aluminum cans, whereas local beer companies used bottles. Ontario had omitted to tax the use of cans for juices and soups, a step that would have affected Ontario producers.

The second problem is generally tougher because it is impossible to find alternative restrictions that accomplish exactly the same environmental results as the original policy at lower cost. An adjudicating panel is then forced to evaluate, implicitly or explicitly, the tradeoffs between the cost in trade disruption and the cost in lesser fulfillment of the environmental objective. It is therefore likely that environmentalists and trade experts will differ on which weights the panel should assign to these divergent interests.

Environmentalists tend to be fearful about the use of scientific tests to determine whether trade in a product can be proscribed. The need to prove one's case is always an unwelcome burden to those who have the political power to take unilateral action. Yet the trade experts have the better of the argument. Imagine that

U.S. growers sprayed apples with the pesticide Alar, whereas European growers did not, and that European consumers began to agitate against Alar as harmful. Should the European Community be allowed to end the importation of the U.S. apples without meeting *some* scientific test of its health concerns? Admittedly, even hard science is often not hard enough—different studies may reach different conclusions. But without the restraining hand of science, the itch to indulge one's fears—and to play on the fears of others—would be irresistible.

In all cases, the moderate environmentalists would like to see GATT adopt more transparent procedures for adjudicating disputes. They also desire greater legal standing to file briefs when environmental regulations are at issue. These goals seem both reasonable and feasible.

Not all environmental problems are local; some are truly global, such as the greenhouse effect and the depletion of the stratospheric ozone. They raise more issues that require cooperative, multilateral solutions. Such solutions must be both efficient and equitable. Still, it is easy to see that rich countries might use their economic power to reach protocols that maximize efficiency at the expense of poorer countries.

For instance, imagine that the drafters of a protocol were to ask Brazil to refrain from cutting down its rain forests while allowing industrialized countries to continue emitting carbon dioxide. They might justify this request on the grounds that it costs Brazil less to keep a tree alive, absorbing a unit of carbon dioxide every year, than it would cost the U.S. or Germany to save a unit by burning less oil. Such a trade-off would indeed be economically efficient. Yet if Brazil, a poorer country, were then left with the bill, the solution would assuredly be inequitable.

Before any group of countries imposes trade sanctions on a country that has not joined a multilateral protocol, it would be important to judge whether the protocol is indeed fair. Nonmembers targeted for trade sanctions should have the right to get an impartial hearing of their objections, requiring the strong to defend their actions even when they appear to be entirely virtuous.

The simultaneous pursuit of the two causes of free trade and a protected environment often raises problems, to be sure. But none of these conflicts is beyond resolution with goodwill and by imaginative institutional innovation. The aversion to free trade and GATT that many environmentalists display is unfounded, and it is time for them to shed it. Their admirable moral passion and certain intellectual vigor are better devoted to building bridges between the causes of trade and the environment.

The Author

Jagdish Bhagwati is Arthur Lehman Professor of Economics and professor of political science at Columbia University and was Ford International Professor of Economics at the

Massachusetts Institute of Technology. He has served as the economic policy adviser to the director-general of the General Agreement on Tariffs and Trade. Five volumes of his collected essays have been published by MIT Press. His most recent books are Protectionism *(MIT Press, 1988) and* The World Trading System at Risk *(Princeton University Press, 1991). He also writes frequently for the* New York Times, *the* Wall Street Journal *and the* New Republic.

In this second article debating the merits of free trade, Herman E. Daly makes the case that free trade has hidden costs to the environment and community, and adheres to a faulty assumption. Free trade makes sense, he says, if a nation specializes in goods it produces more cheaply and efficiently than other nations and can trade them freely to obtain specialty products from other nations.

However, this nineteenth-century notion assumes that a country's capital stays in the country and doesn't subsidize foreign production, because that would disrupt the balanced, mutual relationship of the trading partners. This assumption is clearly violated in the global economy.

"Free trade," Daly says, "has long been presumed good unless proved otherwise." But this

presumption should be reversed to favor "domestic production for domestic markets," using "balanced international trade" only when it is "convenient," and never to "govern a country's affairs at the risk of environmental and social disaster."

He further argues that free trade could be accused of "reverse environmental imperialism" because when countries "produce under the most permissive standards and sell their products elsewhere without penalty, they press on countries with higher standards to lower them." The issues Daly raises continue to be of concern with more recent international trade agreements, such as the Central American Free Trade Agreement (CAFTA), which narrowly passed in 2005. —RA

"The Perils of Free Trade"
by Herman E. Daly
Scientific American, November 1993

No policy prescription commands greater consensus among economists than that of free trade based on international specialization according to comparative advantage. Free trade has long been presumed good unless proved otherwise. That presumption is the cornerstone of the existing General Agreement on Tariffs and Trade (GATT) and the proposed North American Free Trade Agreement (NAFTA). The proposals in the Uruguay Round of negotiations strengthen GATT's basic commitment to free trade and economic globalization.

Yet that presumption should be reversed. The default position should favor domestic production for domestic markets. When convenient, balanced international trade should be used, but it should not be allowed to govern a country's affairs at the risk of environmental and social disaster. The domestic economy should be the dog and international trade its tail. GATT seeks to tie all the dogs' tails together so tightly that the international knot would wag the separate national dogs.

The wiser course was well expressed in the overlooked words of John Maynard Keynes: "I sympathize, therefore, with those who would minimize, rather than those who would maximize, economic entanglement between nations. Ideas, knowledge, art, hospitality, travel—these are the things which should of their nature be international. But let goods be homespun whenever it is reasonably and conveniently possible; and, above all, let finance be primarily national." Contrary to Keynes, the defenders of the proposed Uruguay Round of changes to GATT not only want to downplay "homespun goods," they also want finance and all other services to become primarily international.

Economists and environmentalists are sometimes represented as being, respectively, for and against free trade, but that polarization does the argument a disservice. Rather the real debate is over what kinds of regulations are to be instituted and what goals are legitimate. The free traders seek to maximize profits and production without regard for considerations that represent hidden social and environmental costs. They argue that when growth has made people wealthy enough, they will have the funds to clean up the damage done by growth. Conversely, environmentalists and some economists, myself among them, suspect that growth is increasing environmental costs faster than benefits from production—thereby making us poorer, not richer.

A more accurate name than the persuasive label "free trade"—because who can be opposed to freedom?—is "deregulated international commerce." Deregulation is not always a good policy: recall the recent experience of the U.S. with the deregulation of the savings and loan institutions. As one who formerly taught the doctrine of free trade to college students, I have some sympathy for the free traders' view. Nevertheless, my major concern about my profession today is that our disciplinary preference for logically beautiful results over factually grounded policies has reached such fanatical proportions that we economists have become dangerous to the earth and its inhabitants.

The free trade position is grounded in the logic of comparative advantage, first explicitly formulated by the early 19th-century British economist David Ricardo. He observed that countries with different technologies, customs and resources will incur different costs when they make the same products. One country may find it comparatively less costly to mine coal than to grow wheat, but in another country the opposite may be true. If nations specialize in the products for which they have a comparative advantage and trade freely to obtain others, everyone benefits.

The problem is not the logic of this argument. It is the relevance of Ricardo's critical but often forgotten assumption that factors of production (especially capital) are internationally immobile. In today's world, where billions of dollars can be transferred between nations at the speed of light, that essential condition is not met. Moreover, free traders encourage such foreign investment as a development strategy. In short, the free traders are using an argument that hinges on the impermeability of national boundaries to capital to support a policy aimed at making those same boundaries increasingly permeable to both capital and goods!

That fact alone invalidates the assumption that international trade will inevitably benefit all its partners. Furthermore, for trade to be mutually beneficial, the gains must not be offset by higher liabilities. After specialization, nations are no longer free *not* to trade, and that loss of independence can be a liability. Also, the cost of transporting goods internationally must not cancel out the profits. Transport costs are energy intensive. Today, however, the cost of energy is frequently subsidized by governments through investment tax credits, federally subsidized research and military expenditures that ensure access to petroleum. The environmental costs of fossil-fuel burning also do not factor into the price of gasoline. To the extent that energy is subsidized, then, so too is trade. The full cost of energy, stripped of these obscuring subsidies, would therefore reduce the initial gains from long-distance trade, whether international or interregional.

Free trade can also introduce new inefficiencies. Contrary to the implications of comparative advantage, more than half of all international trade involves the simultaneous import and export of essentially the same goods. For example, Americans import Danish sugar cookies, and Danes import American sugar cookies. Exchanging recipes would surely be more efficient. It would also be more in accord with Keynes's dictum that knowledge should be international and goods homespun (or in this case, homebaked).

Another important but seldom mentioned corollary of specialization is a reduction in the range of occupational choices. Uruguay has a clear comparative advantage in raising cattle and sheep. If it adhered strictly to the rule of specialization and trade, it would afford its citizens only the choice of being either cowboys or shepherds. Yet Uruguayans feel a need for their own legal, financial, medical, insurance and educational services, in addition to basic agriculture and industry. That diversity entails some loss of efficiency, but it is necessary for community and nationhood.

Uruguay is enriched by having a symphony orchestra of its own, even though it would be cost-effective to import better symphony concerts in exchange for wool, mutton, beef and leather. Individuals, too, must count the broader range of choices as a welfare gain: even those who are cowboys and shepherds are surely enriched by contact with countrymen who are not *vaqueros* or *pastores*. My point is that the community dimension of welfare is completely overlooked in the simplistic argument that if specialization and trade increase the per capita availability of commodities, they must be good.

Let us assume that even after those liabilities are subtracted from the gross returns on trade, positive net gains still exist. They must still offset deeper, more fundamental problems. The arguments for free trade run afoul of the three basic goals of all economic policies: the efficient *allocation* of resources, the fair *distribution* of resources and the maintenance of a sustainable *scale* of resource use. The first two are traditional goals of neoclassical economics. The third has only recently been recognized and is associated with the viewpoint of ecological, or steady-state, economics. It means that the input of raw materials and energy to an economy and the output of waste materials and heat must be within the regenerative and absorptive capacities of the ecosystem.

In neoclassical economics the efficient allocation of resources depends on the counting and internalization of all costs. Costs are internalized if they are directly paid by those entities responsible for them—as when, for example, a manufacturer pays for the disposal of its factory wastes and raises its prices to cover that expense. Costs are externalized if they are paid by someone else—as when the public suffers extra disease, stench and nuisance from uncollected wastes. Counting all costs is the very basis of efficiency.

Economists rightly urge nations to follow a domestic program of internalizing costs into prices. They also wrongly urge nations to trade freely with other countries that do not internalize their costs (and consequently have lower prices). If a nation tries to follow both those policies, the conflict is clear: free competition between different cost-internalizing regimes is utterly unfair.

International trade increases competition, and competition reduces costs. But competition can reduce costs in two ways: by increasing efficiency or by lowering standards. A firm can save money by lowering its standards for pollution control, worker safety, wages, health care and so on—all choices that externalize some of its costs. Profit-maximizing firms in competition always have an incentive to externalize their costs to the degree that they can get away with it.

For precisely that reason, nations maintain large legal, administrative and auditing structures that bar reductions in the social and environmental standards of domestic industries. There are no analogous international bodies of law and administration; there are only national laws, which differ widely. Consequently, free international trade encourages industries to shift their production activities to the countries that have the lowest standards of cost internalization—hardly a move toward global efficiency.

Attaining cheapness by ignoring real costs is a sin against efficiency. Even GATT recognizes that requiring citizens of one country to compete against foreign prison labor would be carrying standards-lowering competition too far. GATT therefore allows the imposition of restrictions on such trade. Yet it makes no similar exception for child labor, for uninsured risky labor or for subsistence-wage labor.

The most practical solution is to permit nations that internalize costs to levy compensating tariffs on trade with nations that do not. "Protectionism"— shielding an inefficient industry against more efficient foreign competitors—is a dirty word among economists. That is very different, however, from protecting an efficient national policy of full-cost pricing from standards-lowering international competition.

Such tariffs are also not without precedent. Free traders generally praise the fairness of "antidumping" tariffs that discourage countries from trading in goods at prices below their production costs. The only real difference is the decision to include the costs of environmental damage and community welfare in that reckoning.

This tariff policy does not imply the imposition of one country's environmental preferences or moral judgments on another country. Each country should set the rules of cost internalization in its own market.

Whoever sells in a nation's market should play by that nation's rules or pay a tariff sufficient to remove the competitive advantage of lower standards. For instance, under the Marine Mammal Protection Act, all tuna sold in the U.S. (whether by U.S. or Mexican fishermen) must count the cost of limiting the kill of dolphin associated with catching tuna. Tuna sold in the Mexican market (whether by U.S. or Mexican fishermen) need not include that cost. No standards are being imposed through "environmental imperialism"; paying the costs of a nation's environmental standards is merely the price of admission to its market.

Indeed, free trade could be accused of reverse environmental imperialism. When firms produce under the most permissive standards and sell their products elsewhere without penalty, they press on countries with higher standards to lower them. In effect, unrestricted trade imposes lower standards.

Unrestricted international trade also raises problems of resource distribution. In the world of comparative advantage described by Ricardo, a nation's capital stays at home, and only goods are traded. If firms are free to relocate their capital internationally to wherever their production costs would be lowest, then the favored countries have not merely a comparative advantage but an absolute advantage. Capital will drain out of one country and into another, perhaps making what H. Ross Perot called "a giant sucking sound" as jobs and wealth move with it. This specialization will increase world production, but without any assurance that all the participating countries will benefit.

When capital flows abroad, the opportunity for new domestic employment diminishes, which drives down the price for domestic labor. Even if free trade and capital mobility raise wages in low-wage countries (and that tendency is thwarted by overpopulation and rapid population growth), they do so at the expense of labor in the high-wage countries. They thereby increase income inequality there. Most citizens are wage earners. In the U.S., 80 percent of the labor force is classified as "nonsupervisory employees." Their real wages have fallen 17 percent between 1973 and 1990, in significant part because of trade liberalization.

Nor does labor in low-wage countries necessarily gain from free trade. It is likely that NAFTA will ruin Mexican peasants when "inexpensive" U.S. corn (subsidized by depleting topsoil, aquifers, oil wells and the federal treasury) can be freely imported. Displaced peasants will bid down wages. Their land will be bought cheaply by agribusinesses to produce fancy vegetables and cut flowers for the U.S. market. Ironically, Mexico helps to keep U.S. corn "inexpensive" by exporting its own vanishing reserves of oil and genetic crop variants, which the U.S. needs to sustain its corn monoculture.

Neoclassical economists admit that overpopulation can spill over from one country to another in the form of cheap labor. They acknowledge that fact as an argument against free immigration. Yet capital can migrate toward abundant labor even more easily than labor can move toward capital. The legitimate case for restrictions on labor immigration is therefore easily extended to restrictions on capital emigration.

When confronted with such problems, neoclassical economists often answer that growth will solve them. The allocation problem of standards-lowering competition, they say, will be dealt with by universally "harmonizing" all standards upward. The distribution problem of falling wages in high-wage countries would only be temporary; the economists believe that growth will eventually raise wages worldwide to the former high-wage level and beyond.

Yet the goal of a sustainable scale of total resource use forces us to ask: What will happen if the entire population of the earth consumes resources at the rate of high-wage countries? Neoclassical economists generally ignore this question or give the facile response that there are no limits.

The steady-state economic paradigm suggests a different answer. The regenerative and assimilative capacities of the biosphere cannot support even the current levels of resource consumption, much less the manyfold increase required to generalize the higher standards worldwide. Still less can the ecosystem afford an ever growing population that is striving to consume more per capita. As a species, we already preempt about 40 percent of the land-based primary product of photosynthesis for human purposes. What happens to biodiversity if we double the human population, as we are projected to do over the next 30 to 50 years?

These limits put a brake on the ability of growth to wash away the problems of misallocation and maldistribution. In fact, free trade becomes a recipe for hastening the speed with which competition lowers standards for efficiency, distributive equity and ecological sustainability.

Notwithstanding those enormous problems, the appeal of bigger free trade blocs for corporations is obvious. The broader the free trade area, the less answerable a large and footloose corporation will be to any local or even national community. Spatial separation of the places that suffer the costs and enjoy the benefits becomes more feasible.

The corporation will be able to buy labor in the low-wage markets and sell its products in the remaining high-wage, high-income markets. The larger the market, the longer a corporation will be able to avoid the logic of Henry Ford, who realized that he had to pay his workers enough for them to buy his cars. That is why transnational corporations like free trade and why workers and environmentalists do not.

In the view of steady-state economics, the economy is one open subsystem in a finite, nongrowing and materially closed ecosystem. An open system takes matter and energy from the environment as raw materials and returns them as waste. A closed system is one in which matter constantly circulates internally while only energy flows through. Whatever enters a system as input and exits as output is called throughput. Just as an organism survives by consuming nutrients and excreting wastes, so too an economy must to some degree both deplete and pollute the environment. A steady-state economy is one whose throughput remains constant at a level that neither depletes the environment beyond its regenerative capacity nor pollutes it beyond its absorptive capacity.

Most neoclassical economic analyses today rest on the assumption that the economy is the total system and nature is the subsystem. The economy is an isolated system involving only a circular flow of exchange value between firms and households. Neither matter nor energy enters or exits this system. The economy's growth is therefore unconstrained. Nature may be finite, but it is seen as just one sector of the economy, for which other sectors can substitute without limiting overall growth.

Although this vision of circular flow is useful for analyzing exchanges between producers and consumers, it is actively misleading for studying scale—the size of the economy relative to the environment. It is as if a biologist's vision of an animal contained a circulatory system but not a digestive tract or lungs. Such a beast would be independent of its environment, and its size would not matter. If it could move, it would be a perpetual motion machine.

Long ago the world was relatively empty of human beings and their belongings (man-made capital) and relatively full of other species and their habitats (natural capital). Years of economic growth have changed that basic pattern. As a result, the limiting factor on future economic growth has changed. If man-made and natural capital were good substitutes for one another, then natural capital could be totally replaced. The two are complementary, however, which means that the short supply of one imposes limits. What good are fishing boats without populations of fish? Or sawmills without forests? Once the number of fish that could be sold at market was primarily limited by the number of boats that could be built and manned; now it is limited by the number of fish in the sea.

As long as the scale of the human economy was very small relative to the ecosystem, no apparent sacrifice was involved in increasing it. The scale of the economy is now such that painless growth is no longer reasonable. If we see the economy as a subsystem of a finite, nongrowing ecosystem, then there must be a maximal scale for its throughput of matter and energy. More important, there must also be an optimal scale. Economic growth beyond that optimum would increase the environmental costs faster than it would the production benefits, thereby ushering in an antieconomic phase that impoverished rather than enriched.

One can find disturbing evidence that we have already passed that point and, like Alice in *Through the Looking Glass*, the faster we run the farther behind we fall. Thus, the correlation between gross national product (GNP) and the index of sustainable economic welfare (which is based on personal consumption and adjusted for depletion of natural capital and other factors) has taken a negative turn in the U.S.

Like our planet, the economy may continue forever to develop qualitatively, but it cannot grow indefinitely and must eventually settle into a steady state in its physical dimensions. That condition need not be miserable, however. We economists need to make the elementary distinction between growth (a quantitative increase in size resulting from the accretion or assimilation of materials) and development (the qualitative evolution to a fuller, better or different state). Quantitative and qualitative changes follow different laws. Conflating the two, as we currently do in the GNP, has led to much confusion.

Development without growth is sustainable development. An economy that is steady in scale may still continue to develop a greater capacity to satisfy human wants by increasing the efficiency of its resource use, by improving social institutions and by clarifying its ethical priorities—but not by increasing the resource throughput.

In the light of the growth versus development distinction, let us return to the issue of international trade and consider two questions: What is the likely effect of free trade on growth? What is the likely effect of free trade on development?

Free trade is likely to stimulate the growth of throughput. It allows a country in effect to exceed its domestic regenerative and absorptive limits by "importing" those capacities from other countries. True, a country "exporting" some of its carrying capacity in return for imported products might have increased its throughput even more if it had made those products domestically. Overall, nevertheless, trade does postpone the day when countries must face up to living within their natural regenerative and absorptive capacities. That some countries still have excess carrying capacity is more indicative of a shortfall in their desired domestic growth than of any conscious decision to reserve that capacity for export.

By spatially separating the costs and benefits of environmental exploitation, international trade makes them harder to compare. It thereby increases the tendency for economies to overshoot their optimal scale. Furthermore, it forces countries to face tightening environmental constraints more simultaneously and less sequentially than would otherwise be the case. They have less opportunity to learn from one another's experiences with controlling throughput and less control over their local environment.

The standard arguments for free trade based on comparative advantage also depend on static promotions of efficiency. In other words, free trade in toxic wastes promotes static efficiency by allowing the disposal of wastes wherever it costs less according to today's prices and technologies. A more dynamic efficiency would be served by outlawing the export of toxins. That step would internalize the disposal costs of toxins to their place of origin—to both the firm that generated them and the nation under whose laws the firm operated. This policy creates an incentive to find technically superior ways of dealing with the toxins or of redesigning processes to avoid their production in the first place.

All these allocative, distributional and scale problems stemming from free trade ought to reverse the traditional default position favoring it. Measures to integrate national economies further should now be treated as a bad idea unless proved otherwise in specific cases. As Ronald Findley of Columbia University characterized it, comparative advantage may well be the "deepest and most beautiful result in all of economics." Nevertheless, in a full world of internationally mobile capital, our adherence to it for policy direction is a recipe for national disintegration.

The Author

Herman E. Daly is senior economist in the environment department of the World Bank in Washington, D.C. Before joining the bank in 1988, he was alumni professor of economics at Louisiana State University. He holds a B.A. from Rice University and a Ph.D. from Vanderbilt University. Daly has taught in Brazil as a Ford Foundation Visiting Professor and as a Senior Fulbright Scholar. He has also served as a research associate at Yale University and as a visiting fellow at the Australian National

University. Co-founder and associate editor of Ecological Economics, *Daly has written several books, including* Steady-State Economics. *The views expressed here by Daly should not be attributed to the World Bank.*

Addressing a relatively recent environmental concern that has clashed with trade interests, Tim Beardsley, the author of the next article, discusses an agreement on commerce in genetically modified organisms (GMOs), such as crops that have been genetically engineered to be pest-resistant. The Cartagena Protocol on Biosafety is a compromise between United States–allied food-exporting nations on one side, wanting to prevent a bogus trade barrier, and the European Union and some developing countries on the other. The United States wasn't a formal party of the agreement but helped broker it. Activists say that GMOs could "wreak ecological havoc and cause new allergies," and so must be closely controlled.

The protocol leaves open questions about when a country can ban GMO imports that it suspects could affect the health of its citizens or the environment. In this regard, the agreement gives final say to World Trade Organization rules, which require trade decisions to be based on "sufficient scientific evidence." It provides "modest" controls over GMOs designated for use as food or feed but not intended for "deliberate release into the environment," where shipments would be labeled as "maybe" containing the controversial content. Stricter controls would be applied to GMOs that are to be released. —RA

"Rules of the Game"
by Tim Beardsley
Scientific American, April 2000

In Montreal this past January more than 130 countries agreed on a protocol for commerce in genetically modified organisms (GMOs). The agreement forestalled an all-out trade war between U.S.-allied food-exporting nations on one side and the European Union, together with some developing nations, on the other, but skirmishes are likely to continue. The Cartagena Protocol on Biosafety, named after the Colombian city where negotiations began, leaves unresolved key questions about when a country can ban the import of GMOs that it suspects could adversely affect health or the environment. The biotechnology industry is steeling itself for the more intrusive controls and tests of its products that are likely to be the price for expanded markets.

Although no harm from a GMO crop has ever been demonstrated, consumer anxieties are running at fever pitch in European countries, where environmental groups and newspapers denounce agricultural products of genetic engineering as "Frankenfoods." Activists charge that altered crops could wreak ecological havoc and cause new allergies.

The U.S. has seen much less opposition—perhaps because most consumers are unaware that a third of U.S. corn, soybean and cotton crops have been genetically engineered to tolerate an herbicide or to resist pests. But some signs of dissent have emerged. A bill introduced into the House of Representatives by Congressman Dennis J. Kucinich of Ohio would require labeling not only of GMO-containing foods but also of products derived from them, such as oils. Labeling rules have also been proposed in California.

The Cartagena protocol represents a compromise between the strict controls advocated by environmental groups, notably Greenpeace, and exporters who wanted to prevent countries from erecting spurious trade barriers. On the control side, it allows countries to block imports even if the evidence of danger falls short of certainty. It provides modest controls over GMOs destined for use as food or feed and thus not intended for deliberate release into the environment: shipments will have to be identified as "maybe" containing GMOs, and further requirements may be added over the next two years. A "biosafety clearinghouse" will allow countries to publish exactly what information they need. A stricter control regime requiring "advance informed agreement" will govern GMOs that are to be released.

"The U.S. government and biotech companies have been bullies around the world" by resisting demands for labeling, says Jane Rissler of the Union of Concerned

Scientists. "This is a message that bullying is not going to work." As the world's largest food exporter, the U.S. played a critical part in the negotiations, even though it is not formally a party to them.

At the same time, the protocol does not affect countries' obligations under other agreements, particularly the World Trade Organization (WTO). That body requires trade decisions to be based on "sufficient scientific evidence." So if countries cannot agree on how the Cartagena protocol should apply in a specific instance, a would-be exporter could ask for adjudication by the WTO. U.S. exporters wanted to preserve WTO obligations in part because they require that any limits on trade be proportionate to the threat. "The protocol does a pretty good job of keeping the baby and pitching the bathwater," says Val Giddings of the Biotechnology Industry Organization—the bathwater being, in his view, proposed language that would have allowed countries to ban imports arbitrarily.

The requirement that shipments containing GMOs be identified may, however, put economic pressure on U.S. exporters to segregate shipments of GMOs from unmodified commodities—buyers could decide they are willing to pay more for crops that are certified to be unmodified. New tests becoming available enable GMOs to be detected at low concentrations, so strict segregation laws could be enforceable. Some European countries and Japan have already passed laws requiring that food products containing GMOs be labeled for the benefit of consumers.

But if the Cartagena protocol might slow consumer acceptance of GMOs in some countries, it could also pave the way for transgenic crops to become more widely used in others. Many experts, including Gordon Conway, president of the Rockefeller Foundation, believe that crops improved through biotechnology will be essential to feeding rapidly growing populations in developing countries. Scientists from such countries feared before the Montreal agreement that exaggerated European safety concerns could make it hard for them to gain access to improved crops. "It is completely unacceptable" for European countries to tell developing countries that agricultural biotechnology is not suitable for them, complains Calestous Juma of the Center for International Development at Harvard University, founder of the African Center for Technology Studies in Nairobi.

The GMO crops developed thus far by Monsanto and other companies, though economically advantageous to U.S. farmers, have brought no obvious benefits to consumers, notes bioethicist Gary Comstock of Iowa State University. That fact has limited public support for them, he says, but circumstances may soon change. Ingo Potrykus of the Swiss Federal Institute of Technology in Zurich and his colleagues published in *Science* earlier this year details of how they have been able to engineer beta carotene, a precursor of vitamin A, into rice. More than one million children are believed to die every year as a result of vitamin A deficiency, a toll that engineered rice could reduce dramatically. Potrykus, whose efforts to field-test pest-resistant transgenic rice in the Philippines have been stalled by a Greenpeace campaign there, says researchers in Africa, Asia and Latin America are keen to transfer the vitamin A–producing genes in his rice into locally adapted varieties, a task that may take two or three years. But, he reports, French rice importers have warned Thai growers that they risk losing their European export market if they cultivate the engineered grain. Potrykus calls that threat "a very unfair neocolonialism."

The image problems of agricultural biotechnology have prompted major corporations to end their attempts to integrate it with pharmaceutical development. In the U.S., Monsanto, which has spent billions to cultivate the agricultural biotech market, is merging its pharmaceutical arm with Pharmacia & Upjohn and spinning off its agricultural division. In Europe, Novartis has combined its seeds business with AstraZeneca's agrochemicals division to create an agribusiness company to be known as Syngenta. Industry watcher John T. McCamant, a contributing editor of *Medical Technology Stock Letter*, says shareholders were objecting that pharmaceutical profits were being dragged down by agriculture's lackluster performance and wanted the two types of operation separated.

Still, experts predict that the setbacks will not be permanent. "It's purely financial. DNA and molecules are not going to go out of fashion," remarks Mark Cantley, an adviser to the European Commission, the

executive arm of the European Union. Agricultural biotechnology "is here to stay because the advantages are so compelling," agrees Peter Day, director of Rutgers University's Biotechnology Center for Agriculture and the Environment. And people within the besieged industry say they intend to stay the course. "We are not shying away from the technology," declares Ted McKinney, a spokesman for Dow AgroSciences, which has made modest investments in the field. A new regime for GMOs may take some years to put in place, but the agreement in Montreal means there is at least a basis for making the best of biotechnology's potential.
—*Tim Beardsley in Washington, D.C.*

4 Brave New World

The next article illustrates the perils of letting politics triumph over the environment. It also provides a warning of what could happen today given the spread of nuclear power and weapons programs to countries that aren't accountable to any treaties or international standards.

In 1986, the Chornobyl (also spelled "Chernobyl") nuclear power plant in northern Ukraine exploded. The following article was written ten years later by the epidemiologist and former Ukraine ambassador to the United States Yuri Shcherbak. It is a tale of poor government policy that failed spectacularly twice. The first failure was in using a reactor whose design made it unstable under some uncommon, but not rare, conditions within an inadequate containment building. The second failure was its handling of the aftermath, remaining secretive and allowing contamination to spread outside the country without adequate international warning. Also, not enlisting outside help virtually guaranteed that the plant's hastily built sarcophagus (the tomb constructed to house the nuclear plant's ruined fourth reactor) would not endure many years. Shcherbak writes that Chornobyl was "a global environmental event of a new kind," with "thousands of environmental refugees; long-term contamination of land, water and air; and possibly irreparable damage to ecosystems." —RA

"Ten Years of the Chornobyl Era"
by Yuri M. Shcherbak
Scientific American, **April 1996**

"It seemed as if the world was coming to an end. . . . I could not believe my eyes; I saw the reactor ruined by the explosion. I was the first man in the world to see this. As a nuclear engineer I realized all the consequences of what had happened. It was a nuclear hell. I was gripped by fear."

These words were written to me in 1986 by the head of the shift operating the reactor that exploded at the Chornobyl nuclear power plant in northern Ukraine. The explosion and a resulting fire showered radioactive debris over much of eastern Europe. The author of the words above, along with several others, was later jailed for his role in the disaster, although he never admitted guilt.

Subsequent official investigations have shown, however, that responsibility for this extraordinary tragedy reaches far beyond just those on duty at the plant on the night of April 25 and early morning of April 26, 1986. The consequences, likewise, have spread far beyond the nuclear energy industry and raise fundamental questions for a technological civilization. Before the explosion, Chornobyl was a small city hardly known to the outside world. Since then, the name—often known by its Russian spelling, Chernobyl—has entered the chronicle of the 20th century as the worst technogenic environmental disaster in history. It is an internationally known metaphor for catastrophe as potent as "Stalingrad" or "Bhopal." Indeed, it is now clear that the political repercussions from Chornobyl accelerated the collapse of the Soviet empire.

Because of the importance of this calamity for all of humanity, it is vital that the world understands both the reasons it happened and the consequences. The events that led up to the explosion are well known. Reactor number four, a 1,000-megawatt RBMK-1000 design, produced steam that drove generators to make electricity. On the night of the accident, operators were conducting a test to see how long the generators would run without power. For this purpose, they greatly reduced the power being produced in the reactor and blocked the flow of steam to the generators.

Unfortunately, the RBMK-1000 has a design flaw that makes its operation at low power unstable. In this mode of operation, any spurious increase in the production of steam can boost the rate of energy production in the reactor. If that extra energy generates still more steam, the result can be a runaway power surge. In addition, the operators had disabled safety systems that could have averted the reactor's destruction, because the systems might have interfered with the results of the test.

At 1:23 and 40 seconds on the morning of April 26, realizing belatedly that the situation had become hazardous, an operator pressed a button to activate the automatic protection system. The action was intended to shut the reactor down, but by this time it was too late. What actually happened can be likened to a driver who presses the brake pedal to slow down a car but finds instead that it accelerates tremendously.

Within three seconds, power production in the reactor's core surged to 100 times the normal maximum level, and there was a drastic increase in temperature. The result was two explosions that blew off the 2,000-metric-ton metal plate that sealed the top of the reactor, destroying the building housing it. The nuclear genie had been liberated.

Despite heroic attempts to quell the ensuing fire, hundreds of tons of graphite that had served as a moderator in the reactor burned for 10 days. Rising hot gases carried into the environment aerosolized fuel as well as fission products, isotopes that are created when uranium atoms split apart. The fuel consisted principally of uranium; mixed in with it was some plutonium created as a byproduct of normal operation. Plutonium is the most toxic element known, and some of the fission products were far more radioactive than uranium or plutonium. Among the most dangerous were iodine 131, strontium 90 and cesium 137.

A plume containing these radioisotopes moved with prevailing winds to the north and west, raining radioactive particles on areas thousands of miles away. Regions affected included not only Ukraine itself but also Belarus, Russia, Georgia, Poland, Sweden, Germany, Turkey and others. Even such distant lands as the U.S. and Japan received measurable amounts of radiation. In Poland, Germany, Austria and Hungary as well as Ukraine, crops and milk were so contaminated they had to be destroyed. In Finland, Sweden and Norway, carcasses of reindeer that had grazed on contaminated vegetation had to be dumped.

Widespread Effects

The total amount of radioactivity released will never be known, but the official Soviet figure of 90 million curies represents a minimum. Other estimates suggest that the total might have been several times higher. It is fair to say that in terms of the amount of radioactive fallout—though not, of course, the heat and blast effects—the accident was comparable to a medium-size nuclear strike. In the immediate aftermath of the explosion and fire, 187 people fell ill from acute radiation sickness; 31 of these died. Most of these early casualties were fire-fighters who combated the blaze.

The destroyed reactor liberated hundreds of times more radiation than was produced by the atomic bombings of Hiroshima and Nagasaki. The intensity of gamma radiation on the site of the power plant reached more than 100 roentgens an hour. This level produces in an hour doses hundreds of times the maximum dose the International Commission on Radiological Protection recommends for members of the public a *year*. On the roof of the destroyed reactor building, radiation levels reached a frightening 100,000 roentgens an hour.

The human dimensions of the tragedy are vast and heartbreaking. At the time of the accident, I was working as a medical researcher at the Institute of Epidemiology and Infectious Diseases in Kiev, some 60 miles from the Chornobyl plant. Sometime on April 26 a friend told me that people had been arriving at hospitals for treatment of burns sustained in an accident at the plant, but we had no idea of its seriousness. There was little official news during the next few days, and what there was suggested the danger was not great. The authorities jammed most foreign broadcasts, although we could listen as Swedish radio reported the detection of high levels of radioactivity in that country and elsewhere. I and some other physicians decided to drive toward the accident site to investigate and help as we could.

We set off cheerfully enough, but as we got closer we started to see signs of mass panic. People with connections to officialdom had used their influence to send children away by air and rail. Others without special connections were waiting in long lines for tickets or occasionally storming trains to try to escape. Families had become split up. The only comparable social upheaval I had seen was during a cholera epidemic. Already many workers from the plant had been hospitalized.

The distribution of the fallout was extremely patchy. One corner of a field might be highly dangerous, while just a few yards away levels seemed low. Nevertheless, huge areas were affected. Although iodine 131 has a half-life of only eight days, it caused large radiation exposures during the weeks immediately following the accident. Strontium 90 and cesium 137, on the other hand, are more persistent. Scientists believe it is the cesium that will account for the largest radiation doses in the long run.

All told, well over 260,000 square kilometers of territory in Ukraine, Russia and Belarus still have more than one curie per square kilometer of contamination with cesium 137. At this level, annual health checks for radiation effects are advised for residents. In my own country of Ukraine, the total area with this level of contamination exceeds 35,000 square kilometers— more than 5 percent of the nation's total area. Most of this, 26,000 square kilometers, is arable land. In the worst affected areas there are restrictions on the use of crops, but less contaminated districts are still under cultivation.

The heavily contaminated parts of Ukraine constitute 13 administrative regions (oblasts). In these oblasts are 1,300 towns and villages with a total population of 2.6 million, including 700,000 children. Within about 10 days of the accident, 135,000 people living in the worst-affected areas had left their homes; by now the total has reached 167,000. Yet it is clear that the authorities' attempts to keep the scale of the disaster quiet actually made things worse than they need have been. If more inhabitants in the region had been evacuated promptly during those crucial first few days, radiation doses for many people might have been lower.

The region within 30 kilometers of the Chornobyl plant is now largely uninhabited; 60 settlements outside this zone have also been moved. Formerly busy communities are ghost towns. The government has responded to this unprecedented disruption by enacting laws giving special legal status to contaminated areas and granting protections to those who suffered the most. Yet the repercussions will last for generations.

Multiple Illnesses

The medical consequences are, of course, the most serious. Some 30,000 people have fallen ill among the 400,000 workers who toiled as "liquidators," burying the most dangerous wastes and constructing a special building around the ruined reactor that is universally referred to as "the sarcophagus." Of these sick people, about 5,000 are now too ill to work.

It is hard to know, even approximately, how many people have already died as a result of the accident. Populations have been greatly disrupted, and children have been sent away from some areas. By comparing mortality rates before and after the accident, the environmental organization Greenpeace Ukraine has estimated a total of 32,000 deaths. There are other estimates that are higher, and some that are lower, but I believe a figure in this range is defensible. Some, perhaps many, of these deaths may be the result of the immense psychological stress experienced by those living in the contaminated region.

One medical survey of a large group of liquidators, carried out by researchers in Kiev led by Sergei Komissarenko, has found that most of the sample were suffering from a constellation of symptoms that together seem to define a new medical syndrome. The symptoms include fatigue, apathy and a decreased number of "natural killer" cells in the blood.

Natural killer cells, a type of white blood cell, can kill the cells of tumors and virus-infected cells. A reduction in their number, therefore, suppresses the immune system. Some have dubbed this syndrome "Chornobyl AIDS." Besides having increased rates of leukemia and malignant tumors, people with this syndrome are susceptible to more severe forms of cardiac conditions as well as common infections such as bronchitis, tonsillitis and pneumonia.

As a consequence of inhaling aerosols containing iodine 131 immediately after the accident, 13,000 children in the region experienced radiation doses to the thyroid of more than 200 roentgen equivalents. (This means they received at least twice the maximum recommended dose for nuclear industry workers for an entire year.) Up to 4,000 of these children had doses as high as 2,000 roentgen equivalents. Because iodine collects in the thyroid gland, these children have developed chronic inflammation of the thyroid. Although the inflammation itself produces no symptoms, it has started to give rise to a wave of cases of thyroid cancer.

The numbers speak for themselves. Data gathered by the Kiev researcher Mykola D. Tronko and his colleagues indicate that between 1981 and 1985—before the accident—the number of thyroid cancer cases in Ukraine was about five a year. Within five years of the disaster the number had grown to 22 cases a year, and from 1992 to 1995 it reached an average of 43 cases a year. From 1986 to the end of 1995, 589 cases of thyroid cancer were recorded in children and adolescents. (In Belarus the number is even higher.) Ukraine's overall rate of thyroid cancer among children has increased about 10-fold from preaccident levels and is now more than four cases per million. Cancer of the thyroid metastasizes readily, although if caught early enough it can be treated by removing the thyroid gland. Patients must then receive lifelong treatment with supplemental thyroid hormones.

Other research by Ukrainian and Israeli scientists has found that one in every three liquidators—primarily men in their thirties—has been plagued by sexual or reproductive disorders. The problems include impotence and sperm abnormalities. Reductions in the fertilizing capacity of the sperm have also been noted. The number of pregnancies with complications has been growing among women living in the affected areas, and many youngsters fall prey to a debilitating fear of radiation.

The optimists who predicted no long-term medical consequences from the explosion have thus been proved egregiously wrong. These authorities were principally medical officials of the former Soviet Union who were following a script written by the political bureau of the Communist Party's Central Committee. They also include some Western nuclear energy specialists and military experts.

It is also true that the forecasts of "catastrophists"—some of whom predicted well over 100,000 cancer cases—have not come to pass. Still, previous experience with the long-term effects of radiation—much of it derived from studies at Hiroshima and Nagasaki—suggests that the toll will continue to rise. Cancers caused by radiation can take many years before they become detectable, so the prospects for the long-term health of children in the high-radiation regions are, sadly, poor.

The hushing up of the danger from radiation in Soviet propaganda has produced quite the opposite effects from those intended. People live under constant stress, fearful about their health and, especially, that of their children. This mental trauma has given rise to a psychological syndrome comparable to that suffered by veterans of wars in Vietnam and Afghanistan. Among children evacuated from the reactor zone, there has been a 10- to 15-fold increase in the incidence of neuropsychiatric disorders.

The catastrophe and the resulting resettlement of large populations have also caused irreparable harm to the rich ethnic diversity of the contaminated areas, particularly to the so-called *drevlyany*, woodland people, and *polishchuks*, inhabitants of the Polissya region. Unique architectural features and other artifacts of their spiritual and material culture have been effectively lost as abandoned towns and villages have fallen into disrepair. Much of the beautiful landscape is now unsafe for humans.

The Ukrainian government, which is in a severe economic crisis, is today obliged to spend more than 5 percent of its budget dealing with the aftermath of Chornobyl. The money provides benefits such as free housing to about three million people who have been officially recognized as having suffered from the catastrophe, including 356,000 liquidators and 870,000 children. Ukraine has introduced a special income tax corresponding to 12 percent of earnings to raise the necessary revenue, but it is unclear how long the government can maintain benefits at current levels.

Today the Chornobyl zone is one of the most dangerously radioactive places in the world. In the debris of the ruined reactor are tens of thousands of metric tons of nuclear fuel with a total radioactivity level of some 20 million curies. The radiation level in the reactor itself, at several thousand roentgens per hour, is lethal for any form of life. But the danger is spread far and wide. In the 30-kilometer zone surrounding the reactor are about 800 hastily created burial sites where highly radioactive waste, including trees that absorbed radioisotopes from the atmosphere, has been simply dumped into clay-lined pits.

These dumps may account for the substantial contamination of the sediments of the Dnieper River and its tributary the Pripyat, which supply water for 30 million people. Sediments of the Pripyat adjacent to Chornobyl contain an estimated 10,000 curies of strontium 90, 12,000 curies of cesium 137 and 2,000 curies of plutonium. In order to prevent soluble compounds from further contaminating water sources, the wastes must be removed to properly designed and equipped storage facilities—facilities that do not yet exist.

Cost of Cleanup

The two reactors that are still in operation at the Chornobyl plant also pose a major problem (a fire put a third out of action in 1992). These generate up to 5 percent of Ukraine's power; the nuclear energy sector altogether produces 40 percent of the country's electricity. Even so, Ukraine and the Group of Seven industrial nations last December signed a formal agreement on a cooperative plan to shut down the whole Chornobyl plant by the year 2000. The agreement establishes that the European Union and the U.S. will help Ukraine devise plans to mitigate the effects of the shutdown on local populations. It also sets up mechanisms to allow donor countries to expedite safety improvements at one of the reactors still in use. In addition, the agreement provides for international cooperation on decommissioning the plant, as well as on the biggest problem of all: an ecologically sound, long-term replacement for the sarcophagus that was built around the ruin of reactor number four.

The 10-story sarcophagus, which is built largely of concrete and large slabs of metal and has walls over six meters thick, was designed for a lifetime of 30 years. But it was constructed in a great hurry under conditions of high radiation. As a result, the quality of the work was poor, and today the structure is in need of immediate repair. Metal used in the edifice has rusted, and more than 1,000 square meters of concrete have become seriously cracked. Rain and snow can get inside. If the sarcophagus were to collapse—which could happen if there were an earthquake—the rubble would very likely release large amounts of radioactive dust.

In 1993 an international competition was held to find the best long-term solution. Six prospective projects were chosen for further evaluation (out of 94 proposals), and the next year a winner was selected—Alliance, a consortium led by Campenon Bernard of France. The consortium's proposal, which entails the construction of a "supersarcophagus" around the existing one, unites firms from France, Germany, Britain, Russia and

Ukraine. The group has already conducted feasibility studies. If the project goes forward, design work will cost $20 million to $30 million, and construction— which would take five years—upwards of $300 million. Final disposal of the waste from the accident will take 30 years. One possibility being explored is that the waste might be encased in a special glass.

Chornobyl was not simply another disaster of the sort that humankind has experienced throughout history, like a fire or an earthquake or a flood. It is a global environmental event of a new kind. It is characterized by the presence of thousands of environmental refugees; long-term contamination of land, water and air; and possibly irreparable damage to ecosystems. Chornobyl demonstrates the ever growing threat of technology run amok.

The designers of the plant, which did not conform to international safety requirements, are surely culpable at least as much as the operators. The RBMK-1000 is an adaptation of a military reactor originally designed to produce material for nuclear weapons. There was no reinforced containment structure around the reactor to limit the effects of an accident. That RBMK reactors are still in operation in Ukraine, Lithuania and Russia should be cause for alarm.

The disaster illustrates the great responsibility that falls on the shoulders of scientific and other experts who give advice to politicians on technical matters. Moreover, I would argue that the former Soviet Union's communist leadership must share the blame. Despite then President Mikhail S. Gorbachev's professed support for glasnost, or openness, the regime hypocritically closed ranks in the aftermath of the tragedy in a futile and ultimately harmful attempt to gloss over the enormity of what had occurred.

The event offers a vivid demonstration of the failures of the monopolistic Soviet political and scientific system. The emphasis under that regime was on secrecy and on simplifying safety features in order to make construction as cheap as possible. International experience with reactor safety was simply disregarded. The calamity underscores, further, the danger that nuclear power plants could pose in regions where wars are being fought. Of course, all such plants are potentially vulnerable to terrorist attack.

Chornobyl has taught the nations of the world a dreadful lesson about the necessity for preparedness if we are to rely on nuclear technology. Humankind lost a sort of innocence on April 26, 1986. We have embarked on a new, post-Chornobyl era, and we have yet to comprehend all the consequences.

The Author

Yuri M. Shcherbak is ambassador of Ukraine to the U.S. He graduated from Kiev Medical College in 1958 and has advanced degrees in epidemiology. Besides having published extensively in epidemiology and virology, he is the author of 20 books of poetry, plays and essays. In 1988 Shcherbak founded and became leader of the Ukrainian Green Movement, now the Green Party. In 1989 he won a seat in the Supreme Soviet of the U.S.S.R., where as an opposition leader he initiated the first parliamentary investigation of the Chornobyl accident.

The electric car could put a big dent in greenhouse gas emissions. As Daniel Sperling says in the following article, "Cars account for half the oil consumed in the U.S., about half the urban pollution and one fourth the greenhouse gases. They take a similar toll of resources in other industrial nations and in the cities of the developing world." From his 1996 perspective, Sperling outlines the advantages of electric cars and recent developments that could make them technologically and economically feasible. He also discusses California's zero-emission vehicle policy mandating that major automakers make at least 2 percent of their vehicles emission-free by 1998, 5 percent by 2001, and 10 percent by 2003. In 1996, the state's regulators eliminated the 1998 and 2001 quotas, and in 2002, the program was put on hold after the automakers sued. The program is slated to resume after the lawsuits are resolved.

With the recent popularity of hybrid (part electric, part gas) cars, electric cars are being neglected. Indeed, General Motors (GM) scrapped its fleet of electric cars (EV1s) in 2005, saying it couldn't sell them because the company might face legal problems involving the inability to support the cars with service or sufficient replacement parts. —RA

"The Case for Electric Vehicles"
by Daniel Sperling
Scientific American, November 1996

Cars account for half the oil consumed in the U.S., about half the urban pollution and one fourth the greenhouse gases. They take a similar toll of resources in other industrial nations and in the cities of the developing world. As vehicle use continues to increase in the coming decade, the U.S. and other countries will have to address these issues or else face unacceptable economic, health-related and political costs. It is unlikely that oil prices will remain at their current low level or that other nations will accept a large and growing U.S. contribution to global climatic change.

Policymakers and industry have four options: reduce vehicle use, increase the efficiency and reduce the emissions of conventional gasoline-powered vehicles, switch to less noxious fuels, or find less polluting propulsion systems. The last of these—in particular the introduction of vehicles powered by electricity— is ultimately the only sustainable option. The other alternatives are attractive in theory but in practice are either impractical or offer only marginal improvements.

For example, reduced vehicle use could solve congestion woes and a host of social and environmental problems, but evidence from around the world suggests that it is very difficult to make people give up their cars to any significant extent. In the U.S., mass-transit ridership and carpooling have declined since World War II. Even in western Europe, with fuel prices averaging more than $1 a liter (about $4 a gallon) and with pervasive mass transit and dense populations, cars still account for 80 percent of all passenger travel.

Improved energy efficiency is also appealing, but automotive fuel economy has barely budged in 10 years. Alternative fuels such as methanol or natural gas, burned in internal-combustion engines, could be introduced at relatively low cost, but they would lead to only marginal reductions in pollution and greenhouse emissions (especially because oil companies are already spending billions of dollars every year to develop less polluting formulations of gasoline).

Electric-drive vehicles (those whose wheels are turned by electric motors rather than by a mechanical gasoline-powered drivetrain) could reduce urban pollution and greenhouse emissions significantly over the coming decade. And they could lay a foundation for a transportation system that would ultimately be almost pollution-free. Although electrically driven vehicles have a history as old as that of the internal-combustion engine, a number of recent technological developments—including by-products of both the computer revolution and the Strategic Defense Initiative (SDI) in the 1980s—

promise to make this form of transportation efficient and inexpensive enough to compete with gasoline. Overcoming the entrenched advantages of gas-powered cars, however, will require a concerted effort on the parts of industry and government to make sure that the environmental benefits accruing from electric cars return to consumers as concrete incentives for purchase.

Efficiency Improves

The term "electric-drive vehicle" includes not only those cars powered by batteries charged with household current but also vehicles that generate electricity onboard or store it in devices other than batteries. Their common denominator is an efficient electric motor that drives the wheels and extracts energy from the car's motion when it slows down. Internal-combustion vehicles, in contrast, employ a constantly running engine whose power is diverted through wheels and to turn a generator for the various electrically powered accessories in the car.

Electric vehicles are more efficient—and thus generally less polluting—than internal-combustion vehicles for a variety of reasons. First, because the electric motor is directly connected to the wheels, it consumes no energy while the car is at rest or coasting, increasing the effective efficiency by roughly one fifth. Regenerative braking schemes—which employ the motor as a generator when the car is slowing down—can return as much as half an electric vehicle's kinetic energy to the storage cells, giving it a major advantage in stop-and-go urban traffic.

Furthermore, the motor converts more than 90 percent of the energy in its storage cells to motive force, whereas internal-combustion drives utilize less than 25 percent of the energy in a liter of gasoline. Although the storage cells are typically charged by an electricity-generating system, the efficiency of which averages only 33 percent, an electric drive still has a significant 5 percent net advantage over internal combustion. Innovations such as combined-cycle generation (which extracts additional energy from the exhaust heat of a conventional power plant) will soon make it possible for the utility power plants from which the storage cells are charged to raise their efficiency to as much as 50 percent. This boost would increase proportionately the fraction of energy ultimately delivered to the wheels of an electric vehicle. Fuel cells, which "burn" hydrogen to generate electricity directly onboard an electric car, are even more efficient.

Further air-quality benefits derive from electric drives because they shift the location from which pollutants disperse. Conventional cars emit carbon monoxide and other pollutants from their tailpipes wherever they travel, whereas pollution associated with electric power generation is generally located at a few coal- or oil-burning plants at a distance from urban centers.

Battery-powered electric vehicles would practically eliminate emissions of carbon monoxide and volatile unburned hydrocarbons and would greatly diminish nitrogen oxide emissions. In areas served by dirty coal-fired power plants, they might marginally increase the emissions of sulfur oxides and particulate matter. Pollution associated with the modern manufacture of batteries and electric motors is negligible, however.

Hybrid vehicles (those combining small internal-combustion engines with electric motors and electricity storage devices) will reduce emissions almost as much as battery-powered electric vehicles; indeed, in regions where most electricity is generated with coal, hybrids may prove preferable. The impact of electric vehicles on air pollution would be most beneficial, of course, where electricity is derived from nonpolluting solar, nuclear, wind or hydroelectric power. Among the chief beneficiaries would be California, where most electricity comes from tightly controlled natural gas plants and zero-emission hydroelectric and nuclear plants, and France, where most electricity comes from nuclear power.

These environmental benefits could be very important. Many metropolitan areas in the U.S. have air significantly more polluted than allowed by health-based air-quality standards, and most will continue to be in violation of the law in the year 2000. Pollution in Los Angeles is so severe that even if every vehicle were to disappear from its streets, the city would have no chance of meeting the standards. Many other regions in this country have little prospect of meeting their legal mandates, even with much cleaner-burning

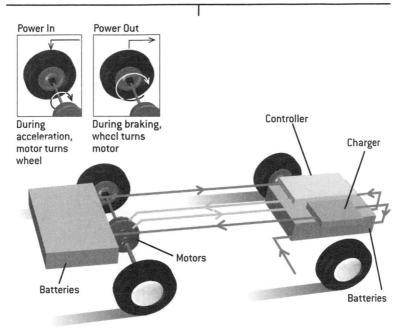

Power In

Power Out

During acceleration, motor turns wheel

During braking, wheel turns motor

Controller

Charger

Motors

Batteries

Batteries

Key components of an electric vehicle are energy storage cells, a power controller and motors. Transmission of energy in electrical form eliminates the need for a mechanical drivetrain. Regenerative braking (*inset*) uses the motor as a generator, feeding energy back to the storage system each time the brakes are used.

gasoline and improved internal-combustion engines. And elsewhere in the world, in cities such as Bangkok, Kathmandu and Mexico City, air pollution is more severe than in Los Angeles.

Energy Storage Is the Key

Electric vehicles now on the market rely on lead-acid batteries charged from a standard wall plug. They are unlikely ever to take the market by storm. Not only are lead-acid batteries expensive and bulky, they can drive a car little more than 150 kilometers between charges. This problem, however, is often overstated. First, there appears to be a significant market for short-range vehicles; second, new energy storage devices are even now making the transition from laboratory to production line.

A regional survey that my colleagues at the University of California at Davis and I conducted suggests that about half of all households owning more than one car—the majority of U.S. households, accounting for more than 70 percent of new car purchases—could easily adapt their driving patterns to make use of a second car with a range of less than 180 kilometers. Many respondents indicated a willingness to accept even much shorter ranges. Environmental benefits and the advantage of home recharging (many people actively dislike refueling at gasoline stations) compensate for the limited range.

Batteries are likely to play a diminishing role in electric vehicles. Among the replacements now being developed are ultracapacitors, which store large amounts of electricity and can charge and discharge quickly; flywheels, which store energy in a spinning rotor; and fuel cells, which convert chemical fuel into electricity, emitting water vapor.

Ultracapacitors owe much of their early development to the SDI's ballistic-missile defense program. Advanced manufacturing techniques can eliminate the tiny imperfections in a conventional capacitor's insulating film that allow charge to leak away. New materials make it possible to interleave a capacitor's carbon and liquid electrolyte much more finely than before. As a result, ultracapacitors can store about 15 watt-hours (enough energy to run a one-horsepower motor for about a minute) in a one-liter volume, and a one-liter device can discharge at a rate of three kilowatts. Ultracapacitors are already available in small units for calculators, watches and electric razors.

Flywheels first saw use in transportation in the 1950s. Flywheel-powered buses traveled the streets of Yverdon, Switzerland, revving up their rotors at every stop. Since then, designs have changed substantially: now composite rotors spin at up to 100,000 revolutions per second, a speed limited only by the tensile strength of their rims. Magnetic bearings have reduced friction so that a rotor can maintain 90 percent of its energy for four days. The first high-powered ultracapacitors and flywheels are likely to appear in commercial vehicles around the year 2000. Because they can provide power very rapidly, they will be paired with batteries—the batteries will supply basic driving needs, and the capacitors or flywheels will handle peak requirements when the car accelerates or climbs a hill. This combination will allow the use of smaller battery packs and extend their service life.

Even the most optimistic projections for advanced energy storage technologies still do not compare with the 2,100 kilojoules stored in a 38-liter (10-gallon) tank of gasoline; for this reason, many researchers have predicted that the most popular electric-drive vehicles will be hybrids—propelled by electric motors but ultimately powered by small internal-combustion engines that charge batteries, capacitors or other power sources. The average power required for highway driving is only about 10 kilowatts for a typical passenger car, so the engine can be quite small; the storage cells charge during periods of minimal output and discharge rapidly for acceleration. Internal-combustion engines can reach efficiencies as high as 40 percent if operated at a constant speed, and so the overall efficiency of a hybrid vehicle can be even better than that of a pure electric drive.

Perhaps the most promising option involves fuel cells. Many researchers see them as the most likely successor to the internal-combustion engine, and they are a centerpiece of the ongoing Partnership for a New Generation of Vehicles, a collaboration between the federal government and the Big Three automakers. Fuel cells burn hydrogen to produce water vapor and carbon dioxide, emitting essentially no other effluents as they generate electricity. (Modified versions may also use other fuels, including natural gas, methane or gasoline, at a cost in increased emissions and reduced efficiency.) Although the devices are best known as power sources for spacecraft, an early fuel cell found its way into an experimental farm tractor in 1959. Prototype fuel-cell buses built in the mid-1990s have demonstrated that the technology is workable, but cost is still the most critical issue. Proton-exchange membrane (PEM) fuel cells, currently the most attractive for vehicular use, cost more than $100,000 per kilowatt only a few years ago but are expected to cost only a few thousand dollars after the turn of the century and perhaps $100 a kilowatt or less—competitive with the cost of internal-combustion engines—in full-production volumes. Daimler-Benz announced in July that it could start selling fuel cell–equipped Mercedes cars as soon as 2006.

Sustainable Transportation

Fuel cells will generally be the least polluting of any method for producing motive power for vehicles. Furthermore, the ideal fuel for fuel cells, from both a technical and environmental perspective, is hydrogen. Hydrogen can be made from many different sources, but when fossil fuels become more scarce and expensive, hydrogen will most likely be made from water using solar cells. If solar hydrogen were widely adopted, the entire transportation-energy system would be nearly benign environmentally, and the energy would be fully renewable. The price of such renewable hydrogen fuel should not exceed even a dollar for the equivalent of a liter of gasoline.

In addition to the power source, progress in aspects of electric vehicle technology has accelerated in recent years. A technological revolution—in electricity storage and conversion devices, electronic controls, software and materials—is opening up many new opportunities. For example, advances in power electronics have led to drivetrains that weigh

Electric Vehicles Reduce Pollution
(Percentage Change in Emissions)

	HYDROCARBONS	CARBON MONOXIDE	NITROGEN OXIDES	SULFUR OXIDES	PARTICULATES
FRANCE	−99	−99	−91	−58	−59
GERMANY	−98	−99	−66	+96	−96
JAPAN	−99	−99	−66	−40	+10
U.K.	−98	−99	−34	+407	+165
U.S.	−96	−99	−67	+203	+122
CALIFORNIA	−96	−97	−75	−24	+15

SOURCES: *Choosing an Alternative Fuel: Air Pollution and Greenhouse Gas Impacts* (OECD, Paris, 1993). U.S. estimates are from Q. Wang, M. DeLuchi and D. Sperling, "Emission Impacts of Electric Vehicles," *Journal of the Air and Waste Management Association*, Vol. 40, No. 9, pages 1275–1284; September 1990.

Battery-powered electric cars, if they were accepted universally, would slash production of major urban pollutants, according to simulations. Pollution from power plants, however, would in some cases partially off-set these gains or even increase certain kinds of pollution, especially in countries (such as the U.K. and the U.S.) that rely heavily on coal and oil.

and cost only 40 percent of what their counterparts did a decade ago. Until the early 1990s, virtually all electric vehicles depended on direct-current motors because those were easiest to run from batteries. But the development of small, lightweight inverters (devices that convert direct current from a battery to the alternating current that is most efficient for running a motor) makes it possible to abandon DC. AC motors are more reliable, easier to maintain and more efficient than their DC counterparts; they are also easier to adapt to regenerative braking. Indeed, the electric-vehicle motor and power electronics together are now smaller, lighter and cheaper to manufacture than a comparable internal-combustion engine.

Every major automaker in the world is now investing in electric vehicle development as well as improvements in less critical technologies such as those underlying car heaters and tires. The resulting advanced components will be the building blocks for very clean and efficient vehicles of the future, but in the meantime many of them are finding their way into internal-combustion vehicles.

Although automakers worldwide have spent perhaps $1 billion on electric vehicles during the 1990s, in the context of the industry as a whole this investment is relatively small. The auto industry spends more than $5 billion a year in the U.S. alone on advertising and more than that on research and development. And oil companies are spending about $10 billion in the U.S. this decade just to upgrade refineries to produce reformulated low-emission gasoline.

Much of the investment made so far has been in response to governmental pressure. In 1990 California adopted a zero-emission vehicle (ZEV) mandate requiring that major automakers make at least 2 percent of their vehicles emission-free by 1998, 5 percent by 2001 and 10 percent by 2003. (These percentages correspond to the production of about 20,000 vehicles a year by 1998.) Failure to meet the quota would lead to a penalty of $5,000 for every ZEV not available for sale. New York State and Massachusetts enacted similar rules shortly thereafter.

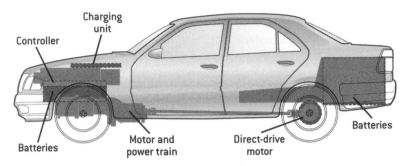

Controller

Charging unit

Batteries

Motor and power train

Direct-drive motor

Batteries

Miniaturization of electronics and advances in batteries and motors have cut the weight of electric-vehicle storage cells and drive components by as much as 60 percent during the past 10 years (older devices are shown in gray in the schematic above, newer ones in darker gray and the overlap in light gray). This reduction has in turn decreased the weight required for the car's suspension and structural components, making it possible to achieve equivalent performance with even smaller components.

The major automakers aggressively opposed the ZEV mandate but rapidly expanded their electric-vehicle R&D programs to guard against the possibility that their regulatory counterattack might fail—and that markets for electric cars might actually emerge either in the U.S. or abroad. Their loudest complaint was that the rules forced industry to supply an expensive product without providing consumers with an incentive to buy them—even though local, state and federal governments were enacting precisely such incentives.

This past March California regulators gave in to pressure from both the automobile and oil industries and eliminated the quotas for 1998 and 2001, leaving only a commitment to begin selling electric vehicles and the final goal for 2003. Industry analysts expect that U.S. sales will be no more than 5,000 vehicles total until after the turn of the century.

One crucial factor in determining the success of electric vehicles is their price—a figure that is still highly uncertain. General Motors's newly introduced EV1 is nominally priced at $33,000; Solectria sells its low-volume-production electric vehicles for between $30,000 and $75,000, depending on the battery configuration. (Nickel-metal hydride batteries capable of carrying the car more than 320 kilometers add nearly $40,000 to the price of a lead-battery vehicle.) The adversarial nature of the regulatory process has encouraged opponents and proponents to make unrealistically high or low estimates, so it will be impossible to tell just how much the vehicles will cost until they are in mass production. Comparisons with the price history of other products, including conventional automobiles, however, suggest that full-scale production could reduce prices to significantly less than half their present level (*see illustration on page 198*).

An Uncertain Road

Faced with the inevitability of electric vehicle production, automakers are devising strategies to produce them inexpensively. Many (including Peugeot in Europe) are simply removing engines, gas tanks and transmissions from the bodies of existing gasoline vehicles and inserting batteries, controllers and electric

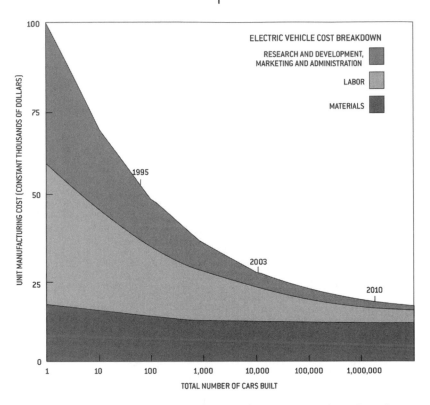

ELECTRIC VEHICLE COST BREAKDOWN

RESEARCH AND DEVELOPMENT,
MARKETING AND ADMINISTRATION

LABOR

MATERIALS

Economies of scale should enable manufacturers to reduce the prices of electric vehicles once production volumes increase beyond their current level of a few vehicles a day. Eventually the cost of materials will dominate the total cost of electric vehicles. (These estimates are derived from experience with conventional vehicle manufacturing, in which a typical factory produces 100,000 or more vehicles a year.)

motors with minimal modification. Others, including Ford, are selling "gliders" (car bodies with no installed drive components) to smaller conversion companies that then fit them with an electric drive. A third strategy is to build very small vehicles, such as the Mercedes

Smart—known popularly as the Swatchmobile—targeted at the emerging market niche for limited-range urban vehicles. Of all the major manufacturers, only General Motors has thus far committed to mass production of an ordinary car designed from the ground up for electric drive.

The cost of batteries (and fuel cells) will probably always render electric vehicles more expensive to purchase than comparable gasoline vehicles. On a per-kilometer basis, however, the cost of an electric and internal-combustion vehicle should eventually be about the same. Fuel for electric vehicles is inexpensive, maintenance is minimal, and it appears that electric motors last significantly longer than gasoline engines. Taking into account the cost of air pollution, greenhouse gases and other market externalities (that is, factors that society at large must now pay for) would tip the scale in favor of electric vehicles in many circumstances.

The challenge for policymakers and marketers is to assure that consumers take into account these full costs, a goal that has thus far been difficult to pursue. In California, where powerful air-quality regulators have led the way toward electric vehicles, progress has been slowed by opposition from both auto manufacturers and oil companies. On a national level, early hopes for the Partnership for a New Generation of Vehicles have foundered on inadequate funding, political infighting and excessive caution. As a result of this internal conflict, vehicles to be built in 2004 will ostensibly have their designs set in 1997, making it likely that the partnership will embrace only the smallest of incremental improvements rather than spearheading the introduction of fuel cells and other radically new technologies.

Nevertheless, it seems certain that electric-drive technology will eventually supplant internal-combustion engines—perhaps not quickly, uniformly nor entirely—but inevitably. The question is when, in what form and how to manage the transition. Perhaps the most important lesson learned from the current state of affairs is that government should do what it does best: provide broad market incentives that bring external costs such as pollution back into the economic calculations of consumers and corporations, and target money at innovative, leading-edge technologies rather than fund work that private companies would be doing in any case.

The emergence of electric vehicles has important economic implications. Whoever pioneers the commercialization of cost-competitive electric vehicle technologies will find inviting export markets around the world. Electric vehicles will be attractive where pollution is severe and intractable, peak vehicle performance is less highly valued than reliability and low maintenance, cheap electricity is available off-peak, and investments in oil distribution are small. Indeed, if the U.S. and other major industrial nations do not act, it is quite possible that the next generation of corporate automotive giants may arise in developing countries, where cars are relatively scarce today.

The Author

Daniel Sperling is director of the Institute of Transportation Studies at the University of California, Davis, where he is also professor of civil engineering and environmental studies. He has written two books and more than 100 articles about electric vehicles and other environmental issues in transportation. Sperling chairs a National Research Council committee on alternative transportation fuels. He is also a member of the National Academy of Sciences committee on transportation and a sustainable environment.

The Endangered Species Act of 1973 has come under frequent attack from members of the public who have run afoul of it, as well as from some policymakers who contend that it's too easy to list a species as endangered or threatened in the United States. Last amended in 1988, perennial attempts to change the act would impose a standard of "sound science," which would give greater weight to "empirical" or "field-tested" data in making listing decisions, as described in the following article. But in the case of rare species, such data is apt to be scarce, if it even exists, some analysts point out. Also, computer models and statistical analysis can

be just as important in making the decisions
as empirical data.

Against this backdrop, a massive fish die-off
suggests that the "sound science" standard needs
to be carefully considered. A decision in 2002 to
divert the Klamath River flow to irrigation in the
Pacific Northwest may have killed some 30,000
salmon, mostly chinook, which aren't endangered.
The decision was based on a National Research
Council report, released earlier in the year, which
said there was no sound scientific evidence that
increased river levels benefited endangered coho
salmon and two endangered suckerfish in the
Klamath. —RA

"Under the Microscope"
by Daniel G. Dupont
Scientific American, December 2002

The Endangered Species Act (ESA), now nearly
20 years old, remains one of the more controversial
pieces of legislation ever enacted by Congress. To
many, it is the most important and noblest environmental law on the books; to others, it is among the
most onerous. Nearly 1,300 plant and animal species
are listed under the act as either endangered or
threatened in the U.S., and powerful legal tools are
at the disposal of government agencies in charge of
protecting them and their habitat. But the use of a
number of those tools depends on scientific evidence—

the proof in the pudding of the ESA and, lately, the subject of much debate.

Critics of the ESA have long maintained that the act's language makes it too easy for a species to get onto the list; they point to its requirement that such decisions be made "solely on the basis of the best scientific and commercial data available." No elaboration on the meaning of this crucial phrase is included in the law or in relevant agency regulations, leaving tremendous room for argument.

In June the debate over science and the ESA took voice before the U.S. House of Representatives' Resources Committee, which met to discuss a bill called the Sound Science for the Endangered Species Act Planning Act of 2002. Supported by Representative James V. Hansen of Utah, the committee chairman, the legislation was crafted to give greater weight to "empirical" or "field-tested" data in making listing decisions. That revision would result in more stringent standards for listing and, when it comes to habitat protection, give landowners more leeway. Hansen called the bill the "first step in fixing" the ESA by ensuring the use of "sound science through peer review."

But what, exactly, constitutes sound science? The Council of State Governments defines it as "research conducted by qualified individuals using documented methodologies that lead to verifiable results and conclusions." But such research may be hard to come by, as two Congressional Research Service analysts point out in a July report: that the species in question are likely to be rare means "there may be little or no information" to be had about them. Moreover, funds for their study could be scarce. Arguing against the bill's attempt to give greater weight to field-tested data is William T. Hogarth. The National Oceanic and Atmospheric Administration's assistant administrator for fisheries says other sources, such as computer models and statistical analyses, are just as important and go "hand in hand" with empirical data.

Hansen's belief that peer review leads to sound science is shared by many legislators, who in recent years have proposed bills that would basically poll scientists for their opinion. But this practice raises questions, too. As the Congressional Research Service report notes, "There may be few (or no) people in the world knowledgeable about some species," and those who are may not be able or willing to participate in peer reviews.

The Pacific Northwest has become the heart of the debate regarding sound science. In 2001, an acute drought year in the region, nearly all the water in the Klamath River Basin was allocated to the river to protect endangered Coho salmon and to Upper Klamath Lake to preserve two species of endangered suckerfish—at the expense of irrigation-dependent Oregon farmers. But in February 2002 a National Research Council report concluded that there was no sound scientific evidence that the increased lake and river levels benefited the fish. So this summer the farmers got their water.

Advocates of stricter scientific requirements point to the initial decision to divert water for the salmon and suckerfish as one of the more glaring examples of an ESA move based on faulty science. Making it harder to prove a species is endangered, they argue, will protect the interests of those who stand to lose if those species are listed and must be protected. Then, in the fall, upward of 30,000 (mostly chinook) salmon died in the lower stretches of the river in one of the worst fish kills ever in the Northwest. Although no one agrees on a definitive cause, some have attributed the deaths to the drop in water caused by diverting the flow to farms.

The sound science act was approved by the Resources Committee in July, but it went no further, as homeland security and the upcoming elections steered congressional debate elsewhere. Those elections, however, may dictate a stronger challenge to the ESA in the next Congress. Robert Irvin, the director of U.S. programs at the World Wildlife Fund, says, "It's a perennial effort for critics of endangered species protection to argue that the implementation of the act is not based on sound science." And such moves, he contends, are often used as "smoke screens for efforts to weaken the ESA."

The Author

Daniel G. Dupont is a frequent contributor based in Washington, D.C.

The United States is notably absent from the list of countries that have ratified the Kyoto Protocol, the international pact that set reductions of carbon emissions. But as David Appell shows in the following article, many states and cities around the country have stepped up to the plate to reduce greenhouse gas emissions on their own. The impact from this won't be trivial. In Appell's article, researcher Barry Rabe states that if U.S. states were thought of as independent countries, approximately 25 of them would rank among the top 60 nations that emit greenhouse gases. In fact, Rabe adds, by itself, Texas exceeds France in emissions.

The New England states and most of the adjacent Canadian provinces have banded together to enact the Climate Change Action Plan. More recently, several other states are in federal court trying to compel some big East Coast and Midwest utilities to reduce their emissions. In addition, a growing number of states require companies that sell electricity to include a significant amount of "renewable" power in the mix. Renewable power comes from harnessing the energy in sources like geothermal heat (extracted from underground steam and hot water), wind, and sunlight. Cities are also acting on their own through regulations, and more than thirty have filed specific action plans with the International Council for Local Environmental Initiatives. —RA

"Acting Locally"
by David Appell
Scientific American, June 2003

Frustrated by federal inaction on preventing climate change, states and municipalities have begun reducing greenhouse gas emissions on their own. In fact, their influence could be greater than that of many countries that have ratified the Kyoto Protocol, the international agreement that set reductions of carbon emissions but that the U.S. has refused to ratify. In the process, the local-area policies are serving as incubators for new procedures and technologies that will be important to a coordinated national effort.

"There's been a remarkable turn of events in the past two to four years," observes Susan Tierney of Lexecon, an economics consulting firm in Cambridge, Mass., and past assistant secretary for policy in the U.S. Department of Energy. Traditional first actors on air-quality issues, such as California, New Jersey and the New England states, have initiated programs to reduce emissions. States are motivated not only by the danger of climate change but by the hope of cleaner air, cost savings from energy efficiency, and marketing opportunities for renewable energy.

Such a "bottom-up" approach has a large global potential: "If they were considered as independent nations, U.S. states would comprise about 25 of the top 60 countries that emit greenhouse gases," remarks Barry Rabe of the University of Michigan at Ann

Arbor, whose "Greenhouse and Statehouse," a Pew Center report, presents case studies of initiatives in nine states. Texas alone exceeds France in emissions.

Rabe reveals a surprising range of situations among those states working to cut emissions. States moving ahead have been successful, he says, in couching the climate change as a more immediate problem, such as New Hampshire's concern over the possible loss of maple trees and the concomitant loss of tourism dollars from autumn's leaf peepers. Many states have a champion pushing the issue, such as Robert Shinn, former administrator of the Department of Environmental Protection in New Jersey. California's historic Pavley Bill of 2002, requiring strict limits on vehicle emissions in 2009, could serve to force redesigns of entire automobile fleets. Sixteen states now require utilities to purchase "green power." Texas, for instance, sells renewable-energy credits and has seen a sixfold increase in wind power generation between 1999 and 2002.

The six New England states (Connecticut, Maine, Massachusetts, New Hampshire, Rhode Island and Vermont) have banded together with five Canadian provinces (New Brunswick, Newfoundland and Labrador, Nova Scotia, Prince Edward Island and Quebec) to enact a Climate Change Action Plan. Written in 2001, the scheme aims to curb greenhouse emissions to 1990 levels by 2010 and then by an additional 10 percent by 2020. (Under the Kyoto Protocol,

Fast Facts: Hot Air

Greenhouse gas emissions are calculated in millions of metric tons of CO_2-equivalent (MMTCE), a measure that adds together the climate warming potential of the different atmospheric greenhouse gases in units relative to that of carbon dioxide.

- Estimated U.S. greenhouse gas emissions, 2001: 1,883.3 MMTCE
- Emissions in 1990: 1,683 MMTCE
- Completed state action plans: 20
- Annual greenhouse gas reductions, 2000: 3.2 MMTCE
- Potential reductions by 2010: 71 MMTCE
- Potential by 2020: 96 MMTCE
- Estimated cost savings by 2010: $8 billion

the U.S. would have had to reduce average emissions in 2008 through 2012 to 7 percent below 1990 levels.)

The first step calls for states to assess the amount of their greenhouse gas emissions; only 38 states have completed these inventories, which account for 87 percent of U.S. emissions. Then, to reduce emissions, planners are focusing initially on "low-hanging fruit," including replacing sport utility vehicles in state government fleets, acquiring more energy-efficient office equipment, and using light-emitting diodes for traffic lights. Seven activities in the region reported emissions reductions or sequestrations totaling 1.2 million metric tons of CO_2-equivalent (MMTCE).

Cities, too, are acting on their own. Thirty-one specific plans have been filed by 141 U.S. members of the International Council for Local Environmental Initiatives, representing 16 percent of U.S. emissions. Ten MMTCE of emissions have been eliminated, according to the council's Susan Ode, in which western cities such as San Diego, Portland, Ore., and Salt Lake City are prominent.

Although individual states cannot replace a federal initiative, their patchwork regulatory approach could compel businesses to seek more consistent, predictable nationwide standards. States, however, often encounter the same reluctance that has dominated the national climate change scene. "We think, whether it's federal, state or local, they're ill-advised policies that are not going to help state or national economies and only succeed in putting more Americans out of work," says Darren McKinney of the National Association of Manufacturers, an industrial trade organization opposed to the Kyoto Protocol.

Still, the collective effort of the states is already beginning to compensate for the lack of reductions by the Bush administration. "You may have some American states that are better prepared, from a policy standpoint, to reduce greenhouse gases than a number of nations that have ratified Kyoto," Rabe comments. The earth's atmosphere will take whatever help it can get.

The Author

David Appell lives in Ogunquit, Me.

Web Sites

Due to the changing nature of Internet links, the Rosen Publishing Group, Inc., has developed an online list of Web sites related to the subject of this book. This site is updated regularly. Please use this link to access the list:

http://www.rosenlinks.com/saca/poen

For Further Reading

Barker, Rocky. *Saving All the Parts: Reconciling Economics and the Endangered Species Act.* Washington, DC: Island Press, 1993.

Carson, Rachel. *Silent Spring.* New York, NY: Houghton Mifflin, 2002.

Committee on Endangered and Threatened Fishes in the Klamath River Basin, National Research Council. *Endangered and Threatened Fishes in the Klamath River Basin: Causes of Decline and Strategies for Recovery.* Washington, DC: National Academies Press, 2004.

Easton, Thomas A., and Theodore D. Goldfarb. *Taking Sides: Clashing Views on Controversial Environmental Issues.* 10th ed. Guilford, CT: McGraw-Hill/Dushkin, 2002.

Gallagher, Kevin P. *Free Trade and the Environment: Mexico, NAFTA, and Beyond.* Stanford, CA: Stanford University Press, 2004.

Keeble, John. *Out of the Channel: The* Exxon Valdez *Oil Spill in Prince William Sound.* Spokane, WA: Eastern Washington University Press, 1999.

Lempert, Robert J., et al. *Shaping the Next One Hundred Years: New Methods for Quantitative, Long-Term Policy Analysis.* Santa Monica, CA: RAND, 2003.

Lentfer, Hank, and Carolyn Servid, eds. *Arctic Refuge: A Circle of Testimony*. Minneapolis, MN: Milkweed Editions, 2001.

Shiva, Vandana. *Stolen Harvest: The Hijacking of the Global Food Supply*. Cambridge, MA: South End Press, 2000.

Westbrook, Michael H. *The Electric Car: Development and Future of Battery, Hybrid and Fuel-Cell Cars*. Warrendale, PA: Society of Automotive Engineers, 2001.

Bibliography

Appell, David. "Acting Locally." *Scientific American*, June 2003, pp. 20–21.

Beardsley, Tim. "Endangered: One Endangered Species Act." *Scientific American*, March 1995, pp. 18–20.

Beardsley, Tim. "Rules of the Game." *Scientific American*, April 2000, pp. 42–43.

Bhagwati, Jagdish. "The Case for Free Trade." *Scientific American*, November 1993, pp. 42–49.

Daly, Herman E. "The Perils of Free Trade." *Scientific American*, November 1993, pp. 50–57.

Dupont, Daniel G. "Under the Microscope." *Scientific American*, December 2002, pp. 24–26.

Galbraith, John Kenneth. *Letters to Kennedy.* James Goodman, ed. Cambridge, MA: Harvard University Press, 1998.

Gibbs, W. Wayt. "The Arctic Oil and Wildlife Refuge." *Scientific American*, May 2001, pp. 62–69.

Gibbs, W. Wayt. "The Treaty That Worked—Almost." *Scientific American*, September 1995, pp. 18–20.

Gore, Al. "24 Hours in Cyberspace." February 8, 1996. Retrieved November 1, 2005 (http://clinton2.nara. gov/WH/EOP/OVP/24hours/24hoursVP.html).

Holloway, Marguerite. "Sound Science?" *Scientific American*, August 1993, p. 20.

Holloway, Marguerite. "Trade Rules." *Scientific American*, August 1998, pp. 33–35.

Kusler, Jon A., William J. Mitsch, and Joseph S. Larson. "Wetlands." *Scientific American*, January 1994, pp. 64–70.

Library of Congress. *The Evolution of the Conservation Movement, 1850–1920.* American Memory Online Exhibition, 1992. Retrieved November 1, 2005 (http://lcweb2.loc.gov/ammem/amrvhtml/conspref.html).

Morgan, M. Granger. "Risk Analysis and Management." *Scientific American*, July 1993, pp. 32–41.

Pearce, David, Neil Adger, David Maddison, and Dominic Moran. "Debt and the Environment." *Scientific American*, June 1995, pp. 52–56.

Popper, Steven W., Robert J. Lempert, and Steven C. Bankes. "Shaping the Future." *Scientific American*, April 2005, pp. 66–71.

Shcherbak, Yuri M. "Ten Years of the Chornobyl Era." *Scientific American*, April 1996, pp. 44–49.

Sperling, Daniel. "The Case for Electric Vehicles." *Scientific American*, November 1996, pp. 54–59.

Index

About the Editor

Rick Adair writes about Pacific Northwest energy policy for a Seattle-based publication. Previously, he reported on government and the environment at Lake Tahoe, the southern Sierra Nevada, and the Mojave Desert. He holds degrees in earth sciences from the University of California–Berkeley (BA) and from U.C. San Diego's Scripps Institution of Oceanography (PhD). He has worked on seismic safety at a proposed nuclear waste repository and on characterizing geothermal resources.

Illustration Credits

Cover © Win McNamee/Getty Images, Inc.; p. 29 Johnny Johnson (Sources: *[left] The World Development Report 1992*, World Bank, Oxford University Press; *[right] Africa's Recovery in the 1990s*, from *Stagnation and Adjustment to Human Development*, by G. A. Cornea et al., St. Martin's Press, 1993); pp. 42, 68–69, 194, 198 Johnny Johnson; pp. 84–85, 87 Roberto Osti; p. 102 Laurie Grace; p. 106 David Fierstein; pp. 189, 196 Michael Goodman.

Series Designer: Tahara Anderson
Series Editor: Kathy Kuhtz Campbell